Susan

Susan

Convict's daughter, soldier's wife,
nobody's fool

Stella Budrikis

Table of Contents

Introduction

This is the story of a woman who had no claim to fame, one of millions like her, who lived her life as best she could, raised a family and then disappeared from history. She was uneducated, poor, cunning when she needed to be, belligerent at times. One man accused her of being a prostitute; her own husband accused her of being a drunkard. She never went to prison, but was familiar with the workings of the police courts both in Australia and in England. Parts of her life are comical, much of it mundane, some of it tragic.

I first became aware of Susan's existence in 1969 at the age of twelve, when my family were about to migrate to Australia. My father's elderly aunt Mill mentioned that her mother had been born in Australia. Her grandfather, a British soldier surnamed Whybrew, had been stationed there, and he and his wife, whose name wasn't mentioned, had given birth to a child before they returned to England. Aunt Mill thought the family had been stationed in Western Australia.

This was the first time either of my parents had heard anything of an Australian connection in the family. My mother, in particular, wondered why my grandmother had never said anything about it, even after hearing that we were moving to Australia. Surely she must have known that her own mother was born there?

Years later, one of my sisters and I both searched the early records in the Battye Library, the State Records library of Western Australia, trying to find more information about the Whybrew family. We found several migrants named Whybrew or Whybrow (the names are often mixed up) but none that had returned to England with a child born in Australia.

Much later, when many more genealogical records began to appear on the Internet, I started searching again. From an on-line forum I discovered that the Whybrews' story began in South Australia rather than Western Australia, and in the process I reconnected with a cousin I hadn't seen since childhood. Slowly, very slowly, I was able to piece together the history of Susan Mason and her soldier husband, David Whybrew. The more I learned, the more intrigued I became.

Because of the vast distance between Perth and any of the places where Susan lived, I did most of my research on-line. Even Adelaide is a three hour plane ride away from Perth. But I did eventually have the opportunity to visit Adelaide, where Susan was born, and Colchester, where she lived for much of her adult life. Both have changed a great deal since the time when Susan lived there. A plumbing business occupies the site where Susan's childhood home once stood in Currie Street in Adelaide, and Colchester has become a town of leafy, brick-paved shopping malls and tourist-attracting tea shops. Even so, my visits allowed me to see the landmarks in Susan's history as real places, and to gain some sense of the terrain in which she lived.

In Adelaide I was also able to look at the original documents of the Destitute Board and the Police Court - large, tattered ledgers with handwritten entries on blue lined pages. They didn't tell me much more than the newspaper articles I'd found previously, but again they moved Susan's story from words on a screen to something more tangible.

For much of the time that I was researching Susan's life I was working in an addictions treatment clinic. I recognised in her many of the same characteristics that I saw in my clients - a difficult childhood, interrupted education, teenage years spent recklessly, frequent trouble with the law, pregnancy outside of marriage, stormy relationships both inside and outside of the family, but a settling down with age and maturity. Coupled with that, a sense of not belonging, of being unable to break into 'normal' society, of being despised, and fighting to be recognised as worthy of respect as a human being.

Susan was, to some extent, my alter ego. I'm a well-educated, well-resourced person from a stable family, with a tendency towards shyness, even timidity, so I found this strong willed, canny, but in many ways impoverished woman quite unlike me. Yet she was my great great grandmother. I inherited many of my genes from her.

I found myself asking impossible to answer questions. What did she look like? No photos of her exist, or at least none have come to light. What kind of woman might she have been under different circumstances? What would she make of her descendants' circumstances and achievements? How much of her story did her immediate descendants know? And how much did they deliberately keep quiet about her?

It would be easy to dismiss Susan as just an ill-mannered, ill-educated nobody, a woman that my parents' generation might have described as "a fish wife". She achieved some minor notoriety, but nothing worth recording for posterity. She may well have been deliberately forgotten, or at least her story whitewashed, by her children.

But all human beings act as they do for a reason. Even the insane have their own inner, inscrutable reasons for their behaviour. I felt I needed to know what drove Susan, what did she long for, for herself and her family? How far did she go in achieving those things? And what stood against her? This is an attempt to answer those questions, as far as it's possible from this distance in time.

It's also an attempt to discover how much Susan was a product of the times and places in which she lived. Her life time spanned almost the whole of Queen Victoria's reign and beyond. She experienced life as a child of Irish immigrants in colonial South Australia, and as the wife of a British soldier in England and Ireland. She lived through the Crimean War, the Boer War and the First World War.

During her lifetime Ireland experienced the worst famine in its history, Australia became a Federation, and steamships, photography and telegraphy opened up the world in previously unimaginable ways. Women in South Australia (1895) and Britain (1918) got the vote, effective methods of birth control became more available, and anaesthesia in childbirth was introduced.

Susan was almost certainly illiterate and would not have been able to read the papers, but she would have heard the news on the street and from David, her husband. She would have seen the changes going on around her. Perhaps sometimes she tried to imagine what life would be like a century after her death. If she could have foreseen the future, would she be pleased with what became of her grandchildren and great grandchildren?

Susan had eight siblings and fourteen children, so her story inevitably includes a lot of names. I've included two charts summarising the Mason and Whybrew families in the reference section at the back (Appendix 1 and 2). Since it is a history rather than a novel, I've tried to avoid offering my own speculation as if it were fact by using "maybe", "perhaps", "most likely" and so on where the facts are uncertain. Occasionally I've drawn on newspaper articles to recreate scenes, including the words people reportedly used, but recognise that these may not be verbatim records.

With regards to referencing, I've debated endlessly with myself while writing this book about whether or not to include footnotes. I wanted to make it easy to read, a free-flowing story rather than an academic history. At the same time I wanted to provide enough references so that others could follow up my sources and check them for themselves. In the end I reached a compromise. As much as possible I've included information about my sources in the text itself. I've also included a list of references for each chapter at the end of the book, as well as a more comprehensive bibliography. The reference section also includes extracts from a historical map of Adelaide.

Chapter 1

Not a little whore – 1865

Life as a Magistrate in the Adelaide Police Court was never dull, and for Mr Samuel Beddome, 23 August 1865 proved no exception. The day, a Wednesday, began routinely enough. As he and the other bench members - Mr Mildred, SM and Dr Mayo, JP - entered the court room, the clerk sternly order 'Hats off!', as he always did, producing a sudden clatter of people standing and doffing their hats.

When everyone had settled, the usual parade of drunks from the police cells began, each hoping that 'Sammy' would forget their previous appearances in his court. Mr Beddome seldom forgot anything or anyone. As was his custom, he fined the miscreants 5 shillings each, about a day's wages for a labourer, and sent them on their way.

Thomas Turnbull, the defendant in the next case, was more fortunate. He was charged with driving on the wrong side of the road, resulting in damages to another vehicle. The magistrates agreed to the charges against him being withdrawn by the prosecutor since he'd paid for the damages already.

The case that followed his, that of Elizabeth Maguire, a widow charged with being a pauper lunatic, was not so easily resolved. Being found guilty of being a pauper lunatic was the legal requirement for a person to be sent to the asylum. Elizabeth Maguire, however, was not in a fit state to appear in court, being, it was reported, completely naked and in a filthy state on a mattress in the police cells. So the honourable gentlemen of the Police Court bench left the court room, temporarily housed at the time in the Adelaide Town Hall while a new court house was being built, and visited "the unhappy woman" in her cell.

Once back in the court room they proceeded to hear evidence from one of her neighbours about her "strange and wild behaviour", which included throwing blocks of wood at her fowls. Dr Mayo duly wrote a certificate for her admission to the asylum.

The entry in the court list for the final case of the day might have piqued Mr Beddome's curiosity. Pasquale Nicro, an itinerant musician, was charged by Susan Mason with "having used insulting language and gestures tending to provoke a breach of the peace". Itinerant musicians who moved from pub to pub and from one country town to another, playing with varying degrees of musicianship, were not unusual. Letters to the editor decrying them as a public nuisance appeared from time to time in the local newspapers. But Adelaide had only a smattering of immigrants born outside the British Isles and the Australian colonies, so an Italian musician had novelty value. What had this young Italian said or done to provoke the wrath of Miss Mason?

Susan Mason, the magistrates discovered, was only a young girl, barely 17 years old, and from her accent more than likely born in the colony. Despite her best efforts to appear respectable and demure, her dress and demeanour immediately told Mr Beddome the social circle to which she belonged. Young women like her appeared before him in the Police Court every day, charged with using offensive language, drunkenness, or indecent behaviour. Still, for her age and social class, she had an unusually determined and confident air about her.

He invited her to state her case.

"Your honour, I'm just a servant girl," Susan Mason began. "I live in Currie Street, near the Ship Inn".

Mention of the Ship Inn immediately confirmed the impression formed by the gentlemen on the bench. Currie Street, in the west end of the town, was where many of the working class, the Irish and the penniless lived. The Ship Inn was notorious for its association with "working girls" and the area had many houses used as "dens of iniquity and vice". It was not a place where Mr Beddome and his colleagues would go for a quiet drink, and they certainly wouldn't take any daughter of theirs to such a place.

Susan Mason continued her story. "At about half-past seven on Wednesday last I was walking down Hindley Street, minding my own business, when this man" - she pointed at Nicro - "not only threatened to spit in my face, but he did so. And then he put his finger up to his nose like this" - she demonstrated the gesture - "and called me a little whore!"

She stopped to glower at Pasquale Nicro, who seemed indifferent to what was being said.

One of the magistrates asked, "Do you know this man?"

"I saw him first at the Ship Inn, where he plays his music," she replied, "but I never gave him any cause to insult me."

To support her case, Susan called on another young woman, Ann Connor, who obligingly agreed that she had witnessed the defendant's "contemptuous gestures and words of the same tendency" (to quote the newspaper reporter's words, not hers).

The magistrates then called on Pasquale Nicro to make his defence. The young Italian appeared to be struggling to understand what they were saying, and eventually they agreed to his calling on a friend to interpret for him. This man seemed to know little more English than Pasquale. As a newspaper reporter later put it, he "vainly attempted to describe intelligibly an offensive interchange of words and gestures."

The gist of Pasquale's argument was that he *might* have used the phrase "little whore", but his English was poor and he didn't know what it meant. This produced a murmur of amusement in the courtroom.

What were the magistrates to make of all this? Despite Susan's protestations that she didn't know the man, it seemed that he knew enough about her to come to an unfavourable conclusion. The two were not much different in age, and he had a certain Italian charm. Had they started a relationship that had gone sour, a case of the jealous lover offended by his girl giving her favours to another man? Or had this foreigner's sense of proprietary been offended merely by what he observed of a young girl's behaviour in the Ship Inn?

And what were they to make of his defence? Clearly he understood enough English to be able to accompany his words with an appropriately insulting gesture. Spitting in a woman's face was a most ungentlemanly thing to do. And yet…

It seems the magistrates felt a certain sympathy with Pasquale Nicro. Or perhaps they thought that Susan Mason was being too coy about the whole affair. No lady would have uttered the words "little whore", even as whispered evidence in court, without blushing. (Only one newspaper, the South Australian Register, even dared published the words when they reported the case, the rest leaving blanks in the text). Nor would any decent girl be wandering the streets in an evening unaccompanied by a chaperon.

They found Nicro guilty of using abusive language, ordered him to pay 10 shillings court costs, but agreed that under the circumstances, "if he promised not to do it again, that would be sufficient". His friend promptly paid the ten shillings and with a polite nod to the magistrates, they went on their way, while Susan Mason was left to discuss the outcome with her friend Ann Connor.

This was the first time, as far as we can tell, that Susan Mason had been inside the Police Courts, though it certainly wasn't to be the last. But who was this young woman, and what made her so determined to defend her reputation?

Chapter 2

From Ireland to Adelaide – 1834-1848

Susan's mother Catherine Murphy was one of many young, single Irish women who, in a combination of adventurousness and desperation, left Ireland in the 19th century to seek a better life in Australia. Though her origins are not entirely certain, it seems likely that she was from Monaghan in the north of Ireland, the daughter of a farmer named John Murphy and his wife Catherine. She arrived in Sydney with her few belongings on 30 August 1840, on board the Mary Ann, one of several ships owned by London-based entrepreneur John Marshall.

Marshall brought over 20,000 emigrants from the British Isles to Australia under the Bounty Emigration Scheme of 1835-1841, receiving £15 per head from the government for each one delivered. Many families and skilled labourers took advantage of the bounty scheme to make a new life for themselves in Australia, but thousands of those who came on Marshall's ships were poorly educated, unskilled girls. Marshall was even accused of scouring the brothels and asylums of Ireland to fill his ships. The girls had been promised employment, but on arrival many of them, especially the unskilled, discovered their only real options for survival were prostitution or marriage.

Twenty year old Catherine could read, but her education did not extend to being able to write. She hoped to find work in Australia as a farm servant. Whether she ever found such work is unrecorded. Soon after she arrived she met a newly emancipated convict named John Mason.

John, a native of Limerick, had arrived in Sydney in March 1834 as a freckled lad of nineteen. He had been sentenced in June 1833 to seven years exile in New South Wales by the Court of Petty Sessions in Limerick. His crime was stealing cotton, probably from one of the ships or canal boats on which he worked as a boatman. It was his first offence.

After spending a month in the city gaol in Limerick, he and two other prisoners, James Quinn and John Scanlan, were taken to Cobh (or Cove, later known as Queenstown, on the south coast of County Cork). There they were housed on the prison hulk "Surprise", a mouldering vessel moored in the harbour beneath the fortifications on Spike Island.

His time in the overcrowded hulk may well have done irreparable damage to John's health. Prisoners were shackled by leg irons much of the time, violence between prisoners was common and diseases spread rapidly among them. Two months passed before the order from the Lord Lieutenant of Ireland came for him and the other prisoners to be transferred to the barque Parmelia in preparation for their exile.

This was the Parmelia's second voyage transporting convicts like John to the other end of the world. She'd been used originally as a troop carrier and in 1829 had also carried settlers to the Swan River Colony in Western Australia. The journey to Botany Bay would take almost 5 months. Among the 220 prisoners transported with John Mason were many Ribbonmen, Irish rebels convicted for their activities against the British and their Irish henchmen. The story of one of these aboard the Parmelia, Hugh Larkin, has been told by Thomas Keneally in his book "The Great Shame".

Once they were boarded, the prisoners were scrubbed, trimmed and provided with clean clothes. They left the harbour on 29 October 1833. Once out of sight of land, their leg irons were removed, and they were able to breathe fresh air and exercise daily, though most of their time was still spent below deck. Perhaps John found life at sea less terrifying than did those prisoners from rural areas who had never even seen the sea before.

Anthony Donaghue, the ship's surgeon responsible for the welfare of the 220 prisoners, recorded that John was a Catholic and illiterate. He also meticulously recorded every physical detail that might distinguish John from other convicts, for future reference and for recognition if he tried to escape.

His notes reveal that John was 5 feet 6 inches tall, with dark brown hair, grey eyes, a slight crook to his nose. His forehead, hands and knees bore scars that could have come either from his work or from some past conflict, but it was probably the leg irons that had left the scars on both his shins. On the inside of his right forearm were tattooed the initials "J M" - his own, or a permanent reminder of a sweetheart left behind in Limerick?

Besides the prisoners, the ship also carried Major Anderson, his family, and a detachment of soldiers from the 50th regiment of the British Army, along with some of their wives and children. The soldiers, on their way to a posting in Sydney, served as prison guards during the journey. This regiment, whose red-coated uniforms became so familiar to John on board the Parmelia, would one day play a significant role in the life of his family.

On their arrival in Port Jackson in Sydney most of the prisoners were sent inland to work as farm labourers. John, perhaps because of his experience as a boatman, was assigned to a prominent local business man and shipwright named Alexander Fotheringham, who leased land off Sussex Street in Darling Harbour.

Some time later John was assigned to Wright and Long, a shipping company with a wharf at Millers Point on Darling Harbour. He may have helped to build the wharf store building at the Point, later sold to Captain Joseph Moore, using sandstone quarried on-site. Working alongside John was another convict, William Doody, a Ribbonman from Queens County who had arrived on the Dunvegan Castle in 1832. He had been sentenced to seven years exile for the possession of firearms. They not only worked together, but also shared the same convict accommodation, and the friendship they formed would last beyond their convict days.

Life as a convict could be hard, even cruel, for those who resisted taking orders or who had the misfortune to encounter a sadistic overseer. Other employees of Wright and Long received harsh punishment for being found guilty of insolence or laziness. But as a prisoner of the Crown, John had food, clothing and shelter guaranteed, something which many of his countrymen might envy. According to the British House of Commons Report into Transportation in 1838:

"An assigned convict is entitled to a fixed amount of food and clothing, consisting, in New South Wales, of 12 lbs. of wheat, or of an equivalent in flour and maize meal, 7 lbs. of mutton or beef, or lbs. of salt pork, 2oz. of salt, and 2 oz. of soap weekly; two frocks or jackets, three shirts, two pair of trousers, three pair of shoes, and a hat or a cap, annually. Each man is likewise supplied with one good blanket, and a pallisse or mattress, which are considered the property of the master."

Many of his fellow Irish ate far less well at home and went about in rags. In fact, rumours circulated in Britain that desperate people were committing crimes in the hope of being transported.

John served his seven years without incident and received his Certificate of Freedom in July 1840, the same year that the transportation of convicts to New South Wales officially ended. By then he had passed from his teens to his mid-twenties and had grown two inches in height since he left Cove. With his precious certificate in hand he could, in theory, go home to Ireland. But like most of those who were transported, he chose to stay. It was not a difficult decision to make. He couldn't afford to pay the fare and there was no subsidy for the return voyage.

He could also marry without having to apply for permission from the colonial authorities. His best chance at marriage would be to find a former female convict, or go looking for a wife among the single girls arriving in Sydney on board Mr Marshall's and other ships.

How John and Catherine met is a detail lost to history. Their courtship must have been quite brief. They were married on the Catholic feast of Candlemas, 2 February 1841, in the wood-panelled Roman Catholic church (later Cathedral) of St Mary, on top of the hill in Sydney. Perhaps they chose that day, a Tuesday, because it was

Catherine's twenty first birthday. She could now marry without needing parental consent. Both Catherine and John signed the register with an 'X'.

There were no photographs - the first photo ever taken in Australia was still some months into the future. Nor did the weddings of couples with John and Catherine's social status make it to the Births, Marriages and Deaths columns of the Sydney newspapers.

They made their home in Elizabeth St, near the harbour and their first child, Rosanna, was born there 10 months later in December 1841. Andrew and Mary Goodwin, an Irish couple who had been the witnesses at their wedding, became Rosanna's baptism sponsors (similar to god-parents). It seems that John and Catherine maintained a circle of Irish Catholic friends around them. One of John's former mates from his days at Wright and Long's shipping company, Timothy Rourke, along with his wife Mary, were the sponsors at the baptism of the Mason's second child, Mary Ann, in October 1842. John's friend William Doody and his wife Bridget (nee Murnane) were sponsors at the baptism of the Mason's third daughter Catherine in 1844.

In 1843 John and Catherine's developing stability as a family was rocked by the death of little Rosanna. Such deaths were tragic but common in the colony as childhood diseases such as measles, whooping cough and scarlet fever arrived with the children of free settlers and spread in the overcrowded conditions in the city. Infants made up thirty percent of deaths in the colony in the 1840s.

The idea of finding a healthier place to bring up a young family may be part of what motivated John and Catherine to leave Sydney. At the end of 1844 they and the Doody family packed up their belongings and travelled together by sea to Port Adelaide in South Australia. They were in effect becoming pioneers. The British settlement in South Australia was barely seven years old. It had almost gone bankrupt just two years earlier. Immigration from Britain had been temporarily suspended, though it would be resumed the following year. At the time of the South Australian census in February 1844 the total population was less than 18,000 people, of whom about 10,000 lived in Adelaide and the rest in small satellite towns. Sydney, when the two families left it, was a well-established city of 45,000 people.

Bridget had arrived in Sydney in 1837 with her parents, Michael and Ann Murnane. A terrible outbreak of typhus on board the ship, the Lady McNaughton, had led to the death of many of the passengers, including two of Bridget's siblings. Bridget's parents had migrated to South Australia in the early 1840s and that was probably the main reason for the Doodys' decision to go there. John and Catherine had no family in Sydney, so maintaining their friendship with the Doodys was no doubt important to them. Several Catholic families had followed the popular Sydney priest, Francis Murphy, to Adelaide, after his appointment as the first bishop of South Australia in 1844, and this may have provided another incentive for the two families to leave Sydney.

Perhaps, too, John and William hoped to leave behind their convict past, which trailed them in Sydney like a ghostly ball and chain. They may have thought they had better prospects of finding work in South Australia than in Sydney. The recent discovery of copper at Kapunda, north east of Adelaide, was creating renewed interest in the little colony in South Australia, while Sydney was still slowly recovering from a recession due to drought and a precipitous drop in the value of wool exports. William came from a farming family and may have been enticed by what he heard about the good, cheap land available in South Australia.

Whatever their reasons, on 22 December 1844 the Masons and Doodys sailed from Sydney on the brig Dorset, along with Bridget's sister Johanna and her husband Michael McCormack. Besides 23 adults and 7 children, the brig carried supplies, newspapers and letters for the colonists in Adelaide.

It was a journey of over thirteen hundred kilometres. The waters of Australia's southern coast can be rough at any time of year, and Catherine, who was pregnant when they sailed, must have found the two week journey uncomfortable, to say the least. They spent Christmas on board the ship and arrived at Port Adelaide on Tuesday 7 January 1845.

As they approached Adelaide on foot, or perhaps by bullock cart, along the road that crossed the mud flats from the port, they would have seen the city laid out in two grids of wide, unpaved streets on the gently rising land around both sides of the Torrens River. A band of uncleared parkland with tall eucalypts and other native vegetation surrounded it. In the distance the flanks of the Mount Lofty Ranges shimmered in the heat haze, mere hills compared to the Blue Mountains behind Sydney.

Coming closer, the two families would have made out several substantial buildings that had already been erected in a classical, conservative style along North Terrace and central King William Street: Government House, the gaol, the hospital, the court house, numerous hotels and the tower of Holy Trinity church.

Looking beyond these they would have seen a few solid stone-built houses scattered among a jumble of hastily erected cottages. These were constructed of either the dark red local brick or pise (mud packed between wooden frames and left to dry) and most were roofed with wooden shingles or even straw. Many of these cottages were already falling into disrepair. Shops, warehouses, factories and workshops were intermingled haphazardly with the houses. The displaced and dispossessed Kaurna, the indigenous people of Adelaide and the surrounding plains, had their own camp in one corner of the parklands.

But perhaps what the new arrivals would have been most aware of as they approached Adelaide was its smell. After almost ten years of settlement the city still hadn't developed a satisfactory system of waste disposal. Human, animal and vegetable waste accumulated in piles around the outskirts of the city. Hundreds of shared backyard privies (unplumbed toilets that had to be emptied manually at regular intervals) added their odour to that of tanneries, meatworks and chandlers, while leaking foul fluid into the river.

Just beyond the west end of the town, on the road from the harbour, a collection of wooden huts known as Emigration Square provided new arrivals who lacked the means to pay for a hotel room with somewhere to stay until they found a place to rent. It was probably here that John and Catherine and their girls spent their first nights in Adelaide, sharing their hut with the Doodys or another family.

On the Sunday after they arrived the temperature soared to 103 degrees Fahrenheit (40 Celsius). They were treated to one of Adelaide's notorious dust storms, whipped up by the hot winds and made worse by the churning up of the miles of unsealed roads by carts and drays. In nearby St Vincent's Gulf the schooner "Hawk" was hit by a white squall, a sudden and destructive storm which came out of a clear sky, leaving it partially dismasted. It was an ominous introduction to their future in Adelaide.

On the same day that the Masons and Doodys arrived in South Australia, a rumour began to circulate that David McLaren, the London-based Manager of the South Australian Company, was promoting a plan to introduce "Parkhurst Apprentices" into the colony. The news was not well received.

Parkhurst, on the Isle of White off England's south coast, was originally a children's hospital and asylum but by 1838 it had become a juvenile prison. From 1842 hundreds of boys from the prison were sent to various colonial outposts, with their convictions pardoned on the condition that they be apprenticed to local employers. The Swan River colony in Western Australia, not originally a penal colony, had already accepted many of them. Adelaide newspapers printed copies of letters between McLaren and George Hall, the Governor of Parkhurst prison, and ran indignant editorials.

The outraged residents of South Australia met on 24 January to discuss the proposal and a number of resolutions were made condemning it. A "Memorial" (similar to a petition) was hastily circulated, to be sent to London on the next available ship. According to a report in the South Australian newspaper on 14 February 1845, within a matter of days it had been signed by 1675 men of the colony. Neither John's name nor William Doody's appears on the list, though they were surely aware of the petition.

In 1845 ex-convicts like John and William did well to keep their past a secret in Adelaide. The colony prided itself on the supposed absence of convicts amongst the settlers. By selling land to those who could afford it, rather than giving it away as in other colonies, and using the proceeds to sponsor free settlers to work for them, rather than using convict labour, the founding fathers hoped to produce a society free from the 'taint' of crime and convict transportation. Until late 1837, a year after the colony was established, no money was even set aside for a police force.

So keen were the South Australians to avoid having criminals amongst them that they transported those convicted of serious crimes within their own courts to other colonies, until this became impossible with the end of the transportation system. Escapees ("bolters") from other colonies, and even those who had completed their sentence, were not welcome. Legislation passed in 1858 allowed for the arrest of anyone suspected of being a convict escaped from another colony. This was extended in 1865 to include even those former convicts whose sentence had been completed within the past three years.

Yet in reality, the colony of South Australia relied on ex-convicts and escapees to do much of the hard labour required to establish a thriving community. Two such escapees, Josiah James Rogers and Thomas Jones, even found work as policemen. The Solomon brothers, owners of the Dorset on which the Masons and the Doodys travelled to Adelaide, were former convicts. Emmanuel Solomon established an import and export business in Adelaide. Many other former convicts worked as stockmen, whalers, road and bridge builders, or labourers like John Mason.

Not only might John have found it necessary to hide his convict history, but he and Catherine would have found their Irish Catholic background set them apart from the Protestant English and Scottish migrants who made up the majority of South Australian society.

Colonel Torrens, later chairman of the Colonization Commission, and after whom the Torrens River is named, had been keen to establish an Irish settlement in South Australia in order to relieve poverty in Ireland. He foresaw something similar to the German colony that was later established in Hahndorf, just outside of Adelaide, but his plans never came to fruition.

In fact, in the 1840s and 1850s, apart from a few exceptional years, the proportion of Irish immigrants among the total in South Australia was always less than ten percent, far smaller than in the other colonies. When the proportion started to rise as a result of established migrants nominating family members back in Ireland for sponsorship, the nomination system was scrapped by the South Australian colonial government.

A handful of Irish migrants to South Australia had the means to buy land or establish businesses, but most Irish migrants came either from the labouring class or were single women (or both). Their Catholic religion was viewed with suspicion by many in the predominantly evangelical protestant colony, though outright bigotry was generally not tolerated. David McLaren, who created such ire with his proposal to bring Parkhurst Boys to South Australia, had been strongly opposed to the establishment of a Roman Catholic church in Adelaide during his time as resident Manager of the SA Company in Adelaide prior to 1841.

In 1855 Irish immigration become an election issue in the contest for the West Adelaide seat in the Legislative Council. Of the two candidates, the liberal-leaning Anthony Forster, editor of the South Australian Register, would probably have been favourite among the Irish of West Adelaide due to his support of universal suffrage, secret ballots, an expanded Council and his opposition to government aid for churches. His opponent, James Hurtle Fisher, a lawyer, was seen as supporting the British government's oppressive policy on Ireland. He wanted to restrict the franchise to those with property in South Australia (thus excluding many Irish residents) while maintaining the Legislative Council at its current size.

However, Forster roused the ire of many Irish people when on 3 July his newspaper published an article which described the unemployed single Irish women who had recently arrived in the colony as "the sweepings of the Irish poorhouses" and suggested that they be given spades and set to work digging in the new Botanic Gardens. Although the quote was taken out of context, it was publicised widely by the supporters of Mr Fisher.

When voters in Hindley Street were obstructed and threatened with violence during the non-secret ballot on election day, "Irish ruffians" were blamed. They were blamed again when a riot broke out later in the day in which supporters of Mr Forster, the winner, were attacked with cudgels and stones. The election was declared void and had to be re-run.

Despite the obstacles John Mason faced, he found work, apparently putting his experience at Wright and

Long's to good use by working as a stonemason's labourer. He and Catherine established themselves among the Irish Catholic community. By 1846 they were living in a two-roomed pise house on Acre 95, off Grenfell Street, east of the city centre.

The house they rented was one of at least 15 buildings on Acre 95, and was owned by a William Peacock. Originally Adelaide had been divided into one acre lots, to be sold for between £3 and £13 to those who could afford it. (This equates to about $3,800 to $16,380 in today's terms, based on average weekly wages.) By 1845, when the Masons arrived, the price of town lots had risen well beyond most working peoples' reach. Many lots, including Acre number 95, had been subdivided, some up to twenty five times, to be sold at a profit and provide cheaper land and housing for immigrants. In the absence of building codes some of the housing was shoddily built and quickly became unsightly slums.

An editorial in the Adelaide Observer of 7 May 1849 described:

"the swarms of small buildings that rise, as if by magic, in every part of the town, and which, from their dimensions and structure, are more calculated for caging animals of the size of monkeys, or for travelling watchboxes, than for the daily and nightly habitations of human beings. A few specimens are to be seen in the immediate neighbourhood of Peacock's-buildings, Grenfell-street, erecting their tiny walls that enclose apartments of an average seven feet by six, in close rows, that give promise of becoming, in due time, miserable nurseries of every description of disease and pestilence..."

Such was the house that was to be John and Catherine's home for the time being. Their fourth daughter Margaret was born there in July 1845 and the fifth, Rose, arrived in February 1847. One room would have been used by the whole family for sleeping, the other as a combined kitchen, living room, and wash house. They would have shared a backyard privy with several other families.

Water for household use had to be transported from the river Torrens by cart and stored in barrels placed outside each house. For many families it was a major household expense. Catherine must have had a constant struggle to keep her family, their clothes and their bedding clean. It says something about her skills as a mother that despite the high infant mortality rate in Adelaide at the time, and the "miserable nursery of every description of disease and pestilence" in which they lived, all of her children born in Adelaide survived infancy.

Chapter 3

Childhood on Currie St – 1848-1855

On 6 May 1848, while still in her mid-twenties, Catherine Mason went into labour for the sixth time. The thin-walled house in crowded Grenfell Street provided her with little privacy. The neighbours, hearing her cries, might have speculated on the chances of her producing a boy this time after so many girls. John and Catherine too might quietly have hoped that they would be blessed with a son. But the baby, protesting loudly at being pulled and pushed into the world so ignominiously, was another girl. They called her Susan.

Her birth went unregistered. Like most Catholic families in South Australia at that time, John and Catherine did not register the births of any of their children with the authorities, even though registration was officially required from 1842. Memories of English oppression in their homeland made Irish Catholics suspicious of any attempt to record and number them or to make them conform. However, they made sure that all their girls were baptised. Susan's sponsors at her baptism on 4 June were Bartholomew McCarthy and Ellen Lennon.

The Mason's house in Grenfell Street was by now far too small for a family with five children, and sometime after Susan was born, John and Catherine moved to a three-roomed house on the corner of Light Square and Currie Street, on the west side of the city. The family moved again in 1852, this time just around the corner to a four-roomed brick house on Currie Street.

The house, on Acre number 130, stood almost opposite the Ship Inn on Acre 120. (Today a plumbing supplies business stands on the site of the house, and the Ship Inn, later renamed the Bedford, has long since been demolished.) The house was the largest and most solid that the Mason family ever lived in, though it must still have been quite crowded.

As was the case in Grenfell Street, a lot of the housing in Currie Street was substandard. On 12 August 1848, the Adelaide Observer reported the recent demolition of a hovel in Currie Street following the death of an Irish immigrant who had been living there. The unfortunate man had died from an attack of "brain fever", presumably some sort of meningitis or encephalitis. The doctor who attended him said he had never seen "a more forlorn and dismal habitation in any part of the world."

The man's sick wife and child were rescued from their dismal situation by compassionate neighbours, led by Mrs Pain from the Ship Inn. Money was donated for their needs and they were found a clean and dry place to live. The newspaper decried the lack of decent housing for new migrants in what was becoming a wealthy colony and called on the government to do something about it.

Cheap, run-down housing not only fostered disease but also tended to attract undesirable neighbours, and the area around the Ship Inn and Light Square was notorious for its brothels and criminal activities. In a letter to the editor of the Adelaide Times in June 1851 a correspondent signing himself as "A working man" of Currie Street complained that the previous evening no fewer than four people were attacked and robbed in that street between the Ship Inn and the corner in a matter of two hours. "I am sure you will agree with me in thinking, that the poor industrious man, who can with difficulty provide for his family, should obtain some additional protection to what he is afforded at present", he wrote.

Fires were another frequent menace in Adelaide's early days, and could spread rapidly through the crowded, poorly built workers' cottages and shops. One such fire in July 1852 brought John and Catherine Mason some short-lived fame.

The story began when the teenage daughter of a widow named Mrs Wyburn went missing from her home in Currie St. The girl failed to return home for several days and her distraught mother searched the neighbourhood, asking everyone she met for news of her. Eventually, to her horror, the mother found her daughter in one of the local brothels.

Perhaps the fatherless girl had fallen for false promises of love and protection. Or perhaps she was enjoying having a little money to spend on herself for the first time in her impoverished life. Whatever the case, despite the mother's pleas, the girl refused to come home.

Mrs Wyburn returned home overwhelmed with emotion. Her neighbour, a Mrs Mason (no first name given), seeing the state she was in, made her some tea and did whatever she could to help ease her distress. It was mid-winter and Mrs Mason left Mrs Wyburn sitting by the fire, shivering with cold and grief but more composed.

During the night Mrs Mason heard screams coming from Mrs Wyburn's house. She shook her husband awake and begged him to find out what was happening. He hastily pulled on some clothes and stumbled outside into the cold.

On entering the house, Mr Mason found Mrs Wyburn screaming in agony on the floor near the hearth, with her clothing almost consumed by flames. He began beating out the fire with whatever he could find, and as other startled neighbours appeared at the door he urged them to send for a doctor.

The nearest doctor was not far away. Dr Baruh co-owned a street dispensary near the Ship Inn, which also served as a consulting room. He arrived, blinking and shivering in the cold night air. After examining Mrs Wyburn and applying what first aid he could, he ordered that she be taken immediately to the Hospital. A Mr Gilbert who lived nearby provided his cart to take her there.

Reporting on 2 August what had happened that night, the South Australian Register noted that Mrs Wyburn was known to be epileptic and surmised that in her grief over her daughter's situation she must have fitted and fallen into the fire. Mr Mason was commended for having saved her from certain death by his quick action and humanity.

Initially Mrs Wyburn wasn't expected to survive her injuries, but the newspaper was able to report that she was recovering, though still "overwhelmed with affliction at the seduction of her daughter". While the daughter was initially said to be 16 years old, the reporter had been informed that she might be no more than 13.

Could this mother and daughter be the same widow and child mentioned previously, who were rescued from their hovel in Currie Street after the husband died of a 'brain fever'? If the mother had suffered from the same brain infection as her husband, she could well have been left with epilepsy.

Although neither Mr nor Mrs Mason's first names are mentioned in the newspaper report, it's highly likely that they were John and Catherine. Several Mason families lived in Adelaide at the time, but John Mason is the only Mason whose name appears in Currie St on the rate assessment books of this period.

At the time of the fire, Catherine had only recently given birth to Jane (born 6 July 1852). With seven children of her own at home, including a new baby still on the breast, her heart would surely have gone out to this poor woman who had lost her only child to such a dreadful situation.

John Mason must have been hailed as a hero by his neighbours. Not only had he saved Mrs Wyburn from a terrible death, but he had undoubtedly saved the whole neighbourhood from going up in flames.

Susan had just turned four years old at the time. Perhaps during the day she had watched her mother ministering to Mrs Wyburn in her practical Irish way, making tea and washing dishes. Perhaps as she and her sisters lay in bed together they were woken by the woman's screams and the sound of men's voices shouting in the night. No doubt she heard her father being talked about as a hero for his quick action.

Though she may not have understood anything of the circumstances, she must also have heard whispered rumours, or even loudly discussed disapproval, of the daughter and the "house of ill repute" in which she lived. The drama must have left a lasting memory.

Susan received little if any formal education. All the evidence from later records such as census returns suggest that, though not totally illiterate, she could barely write or spell, and she had difficulty reading. School attendance did not become compulsory for all children in South Australia until 1875, and even then long absences were overlooked. Perhaps Susan and her sisters sporadically attended the parish school of St Patrick, in the building on the corner of West Terrace and Groot Street that also served as a church. Or perhaps Catherine tried to pass on what she knew.

It would have been Catherine who taught Susan to sew and mend. In 1850s Adelaide even the best-resourced families threw nothing away that could be re-used or re-purposed, and it's likely that some of the clothes that Susan and her sisters wore had been created by the resourceful Catherine from the calico bags in which flour and other products were sold. Clothes were patched and mended and passed down from one child to the next.

Perhaps Susan sometimes gazed at the displays of dresses and bonnets, parasols, gloves, and silk stockings in the drapers' shops in Rundle and Hindley Streets, all confidently advertised as "the very latest in European fashion", "newly arrived on the last ship", and dreamed of wearing clothes like that one day.

As she grew up Susan would have acquired the accent and vocabulary of her peers. Idiomatic Australian pronunciation of English spread rapidly and fairly uniformly among those born in the colonies, from its origins among the convicts in early colonial New South Wales. It was melded primarily from the accents and slang of south eastern England and Ireland, and it was scorned by the well-educated.

Susan must have been well aware of her Irish background. Not only were her parents Irish, but many, if not most, of those who she encountered each day were Irish immigrants or their children. She would have soon learned that being Catholic and Irish was not deemed an advantage by the larger society in which she lived. She might also have come to share the scorn the Irish held for hypocritical English politeness.

It is unlikely however that Susan was aware, as she was growing up, that her father had been transported from Ireland as a convict. Among the impoverished Catholic community in which she lived, having a criminal record was no doubt viewed with more tolerance than it would have been among the evangelical English community of Adelaide. Receiving a prison sentence was likely associated in the minds of her own social milieu with hardship as much as with moral disapproval. But it would still not be wise for a former convict to have his history revealed by an unwitting child. Such information was far too damaging to be shared with a young child who might inadvertently tell the wrong people.

As Christmas 1855 approached, the Mason family ranged in age from Mary Ann at 13 to baby Bridget, aged 18 months. The two oldest girls, Mary Ann and Catherine (aged 11) were both working as servant girls, bringing in a few shillings each week for working 14 hour days. With much hard work and perseverance the Mason family had prospects of improving their lot.

Some of their neighbours had already saved enough to buy properties of their own and had moved on. Their friends William and Bridget Doody had taken up a farm on the Gawler plains and were doing well. It is probably significant that William could read and write. He was able to read the newspapers and keep abreast of prices and opportunities, whereas John Mason had to rely on others to keep him informed.

Nevertheless, John had successfully inched his way into a wider circle of Adelaide society. Some time in the 1850s he joined the Ancient Order of Foresters, one of several Friendly Societies that existed in South Australia at the time. Perhaps he was encouraged to do so by one of his neighbours, Mr Pain, the owner of the Ship Inn, or Dr Baruh, both of whom belonged to the order. Members of these societies each contributed a levy, a small amount of money paid regularly, which was then invested. If they died, the Order paid for their funeral and provided money to help their widows and children get through the initial hardship of losing a breadwinner.

The Foresters were not a Masonic order, although like the Freemasons they had their own rituals. They provided companionship and social interaction among men as well as mutual aid. Members came from all religious denominations, social classes and levels of education. Local groups were known as Courts, each with its own fanciful name, and these belonged to larger Districts. John belonged to the Court Perseverance.

One Wednesday evening late in October 1855, the Court Perseverance met in the (now demolished) Prince of Wales hotel in Angas St, Adelaide for their anniversary dinner. After a meal which "for abundance and variety of delicacies, for exquisite cookery and choice wines, would bear favourable comparison with some of the crack hotels of the mother country" according to the Adelaide Observer on 3 November, they got down to the important business of proposing the loyal toasts.

After singing the National Anthem, they toasted Her Majesty's health and then the health of Prince Albert and the rest of the Royal Family, each toast being accompanied by a song from one of the Brothers. Next they drank a toast to the Governor, and then to the Army and Navy. Someone proposed a toast to the High Court and Executive Council of the Ancient Order of Foresters. This was drunk "with the Forester's fire", which presumably means enthusiastically.

Then, perhaps emboldened by alcohol, Brother John Mason got up. He had no toast to propose, but immediately began a song, "The White Squall", carefully navigating the complexities of the tune with its dramatic changes of tempo and key:

The sea was bright and the bark rode well,
The breeze bore the tone of the vesper bell:
'Twas a gallant bark, with crew as brave,
As ever launched on the heaving wave.
She shone in the light of declining day,
And each sail was set and each heart was gay.

They neared the land where in beauty smiles
The sunny shores of the Grecian isles:
All thought of home, of that welcome dear,
Which soon should greet each wanderer's ear.
And in fancy joined the social throng,
In the festive dance and the joyous song.

A white cloud glides thro' the azure sky,
What means that wild despairing cry?
Farewell, the visioned scenes of home!
That cry is Help! where no help can come.

For the White Squall rides on the surging wave,
And the bark is gulphed in an ocean grave.

The song, composed by George Barker, was popular at the time, and that may be why John sang it. It was also hauntingly prescient. Perhaps when he joined the Foresters John already had some premonition of what was to come, or felt some symptoms of the illness about to strike him. This was the last such meeting that he would ever attend.

Chapter 4

Destitute – 1856-1860

Early in 1856 John became ill - so ill that he was unable to work or even get out of bed. For nine months he lay at home, while Catherine struggled to clothe and feed her girls as well as care for him. Neighbours and friends did what they could to help. Eleven year old Margaret went out to work and added her small wages to the family income. Perhaps the Ancient Order of Foresters contributed some assistance. But in the end Catherine could no longer put off the awful moment. In November 1856 she approached the Destitute Board for help.

In the early days of the colony the Emigration Agent had been responsible for any cases of need. In 1849 the Destitute Board of South Australia was created to manage government assistance to those who had no other means of support. It was, in a sense, an admission of defeat for those who believed that, by stocking the colony with the right mix of capitalist land owners and virtuous labour, both poverty and crime could be avoided.

The number of people supported by the Destitute Board varied from year to year. According to the Adelaide Times of 14 July 1857, 327 people were on the books on 30 June; 119 of these for "indoor relief" in the Destitute Asylum, 191 on "outdoor relief" outside the Asylum, and 17 in country towns.

The Destitute Asylum, in Kintore Avenue, was an option that Catherine surely hoped to avoid. It was intended as a place of last resort for those who had nowhere else to go. This included unmarried women in the final stages of pregnancy. Behind its high bluestone walls, men, women and children were kept segregated, and were allowed to leave the building for only a few hours once a week. They were expected to work for their keep, and to wear the distinctive uniform, even when they went out. Conditions were deliberately made harsh to deter people from seeking assistance.

From its beginning in 1849 the Board required that applicants for any form of relief make a "declaration of destitution" along with supplying personal details such as their occupation, the ages of their children, and the date and means of their arrival in the colony. They also had to provide the names of other family members in the colony who might provide assistance, as was required under an act passed in 1843. Members of the all-male Board, which met weekly on Mondays, included clergymen, the Colonial Surgeon, and the Emigration Agent.

Constant debate arose in the colony over whether or not the Board showed adequate (or even excessive) charity and compassion to those on its books. An editorial in the Adelaide Observer on April 11 1857 gives a taste of this debate:

The Dean of Adelaide reiterates [...] that theDestitute Board ought not to dispense charity.To save from absolute destitution is, in his view, the only legitimate function of the Board.But we may ask the rev. gentleman to define"destitution." What is it? Is a person outof employment destitute? Is a person incapacitated for work destitute? Are people destitute so long as they have an article of furniture, or of personal property, by the sale of which they might raise a loaf of bread? Is aperson destitute who has a friend not destitute?Is destitution synonymous with starvation?It is exceedingly desirable that we should knowwhat is regarded as "destitution" by the Destitute Board; and also that we should knowon what principle we can relieve "destitution" and not bestow "charity".

It was to this formidable body that Catherine Mason had to make her application for help to feed her family. The minutes of the Destitute Board on 21 November 1856 detail the information provided by Catherine, under John's name, "Jno. Mason (sic), Currie St". His occupation as a labourer, the number and ages of the children, and his nine months' inability to work were recorded. The family's arrival in Adelaide on the Dorset in 1845 was noted, and perhaps thus the question of John's deeper past was avoided. A Dr Sholl is mentioned as supporting the family's application for relief.

Under "other comments" the record says that John was English. How this information was obtained isn't recorded. Did Catherine provide it? John, coming from a city with a port, could possibly have been the son of an English sailor or boatman like himself, though other records clearly say he was a native of Limerick. Perhaps it was simply a clerical error. His name may have suggested an English origin to someone who didn't know him.

Unfortunately neither the Destitute Board record, nor the newspaper reports of their meeting, say anything about the nature of John's illness. He was never admitted to hospital, or mentioned in the newspapers as the victim of a mishap, so an accident or work-related injury seems unlikely. He may have had a chronic infectious illness such as tuberculosis or rheumatic fever, both of which were prevalent in Adelaide at the time and common amongst former convicts, especially those from Ireland. Conditions which today can be treated readily with medications were often debilitating in the past. He evidently suffered at home, and would have had to rely on charity to pay for any medical care he received.

Whatever the nature of the problem, the Destitute Board members decided to send someone to see him to check out the facts. They must have done this immediately, because on the same date, 21 November, a second entry for John appears, with all the same details except for a slight adjustment to the ages of the children. It records that the family was provided with "outdoor relief" of two rations, meaning that they avoided being admitted to the Destitute Asylum. That, at least, must have been some relief to Catherine.

But John did not recover. Christmas 1856 would have been bleak for the whole family, with little money to buy what was necessary, let alone celebrate the feast, and little reason for celebration. Then, on 22 January, John died. He was 42 years old.

No doubt the Catholic community rallied to help Catherine and provide whatever comfort they could. Michael Murnane, Bridget Doody's father, registered John's death on Catherine's behalf. Few details were required, just his age, occupation and place of residence, which was simply "Adelaide". Cause of death was said to be "Disease of the heart", but it's unclear whether this was what had left him bed-bound for 12 months or merely what delivered the final blow.

Someone paid for a brief death notice to be placed in the Adelaide Times: "Died - On Thursday, 22nd January, Mr John Mason, of Currie-St west, aged 43 years (sic). The deceased leaves a widow and eight children." The Ancient Order of Foresters inserted a notice in The Adelaide Times on Friday, the day after John's death, requesting that the Brethren attend his funeral that same day at 4.00pm. In an era without refrigeration, burials necessarily followed death as quickly as possible. The Order would no doubt have paid the funeral expenses. Where John was buried is a mystery. His name doesn't appear in the register of the West Terrace cemetery, the most usual place of burial for residents of west Adelaide at the time.

The widowed Catherine, with her eight children, found herself in a dire situation. With two children, Jane and Bridget, still toddlers, she couldn't go out to work, though she may have taken in washing or sewing to earn a small amount. Charity from friends, the Foresters' pay-out, plus the older girls' earnings apparently kept the family above water for the six months until June 1857. Then Catherine was forced to return to the Destitute Board to plead once more for relief.

The newspaper reporter from the South Australian Register, present at the Board's meeting, noted that the three older girls, aged 14, 13, and 11, earned "14s (shillings) and board". A labourer in South Australia could earn 6s 9d per day in 1856, or about 40 shillings (£2) per six day week, while a female domestic servant earned about 6 shillings per week plus board. The three girls together thus earned in a week what John might have earned in two days.

In June the Board agreed to provide Catherine with two rations. If a ration in 1857 was the same as it had been six years previously, in 1851, a single ration for an adult female consisted of 20oz (about 570g) of flour, 4½ oz (about 125g) of meat, 1¼ oz (30g) of sugar, ½ oz (15g) of tea, ¼ oz (7g) of salt, and ¼ oz (7g) of soap daily. The Board continued this provision in January 1858 and then again in March 1858, by which time 11 year old Rose had also begun work as a servant girl. Catherine's name appears again in newspaper accounts of the Board's meetings in August 1859, and for the final time in December 1859, two years after John's death. Catherine's situation during this time must have been extreme to be able to persuade the members of the Destitute Board of her need. Many applicants in apparently similar circumstances had their applications refused.

Susan was eight years old when her father died. Whatever John had been to her as a father - kind or stern, involved or distracted, fun-loving or sombre - he was now gone.

As a child of an impoverished family, with little or no education, she was in a vulnerable position. She had no father, brother or uncles to support or protect her, either from poverty or from exploitation. In a society where even adult women had the same legal status as children, and gained much of their social status from their male guardians, having no male family member was a severe disadvantage. In time South Australia would lead the world in giving women equal rights with men, not just politically, but in access to education and employment. But for now, Susan and her sisters were close to the bottom of the social heap.

At the same time, as a member of an all-female family she learned through experience that it was possible for women to survive without a man's support. She observed her mother Catherine's struggle to avoid having her family broken up or consigned to the Destitute Asylum. The same strength of mind and character that had once taken Catherine half way across the world to start a new life in Australia gave her determination and endurance now.

Perhaps Susan was born with that same fighting spirit and a shrewd mind. And no doubt as a middle child she had no option but to learn to stand up for herself, not only to survive but also to avoid being overlooked.

With her four older sisters spending most of the week in the houses where they worked, and her mother preoccupied with looking after the two youngest children and trying to make ends meet, she and her younger sister Eliza probably went unsupervised much of the time. They had to entertain themselves.

After doing any chores set for them by Catherine, they might have played hopscotch or tag in the street with the neighbouring children. Tiring of that, they could have sat, barefoot, outside the house on Currie St, and watched the horse-drawn carts delivering goods to the nearby warehouses and shops. Water was still being carted from the river in tanks in those days. They would have seen people carrying parcels along the street or visiting Dr Baruh's dispensary across the road.

In summer the passing carts stirred up the dust on the unpaved road and added their rattle to the clanging and hammering coming from the blacksmiths and other workshops around. In winter the cart wheels churned up the mud, leaving deep ruts that filled with water.

At the right time of day Susan and Eliza would have smelled the bread baking in the bakery a few doors up the street, or, if the wind was from the wrong direction, the smell of hen houses, pig-sties and privies in the yards behind the houses. It was not uncommon to see a stray chicken, pig or goat wandering the street, soon to be chased by a policeman and amused onlookers.

Perhaps they watched the comings and goings from the nearby Ship Inn. They could have stood at the door and listened to the music being played by travelling musicians like Pasquale Nicro, or even crept inside to get a better view. No doubt they would have seen girls coming out of the Ship Inn, or one of the many other public houses in the street, clutching the arms of tipsy men, laughing and joking together, before they disappeared into the doorway of a nearby hovel.

By the time she was eleven years old Susan would have been expected to find employment as a servant girl like her sisters. She may even have worked at the Ship Inn, cleaning rooms, washing sheets, cooking and running errands under the supervision of Mrs Pain. Her childhood was over.

Chapter 5

Life on the streets – 1860-1867

Susan's appearance in court in August 1865, as the plaintiff against Pasquale Nicro, came in the midst of an eventful year for the Mason family. In June her older sister Catherine married George Davis, a locally born labourer. The newly married couple moved to Port Adelaide and their first child was born the following January.

In July her eldest sister Mary Ann married Henry Atkin, the son of the Masons' widowed next door neighbour, also named Henry. Mary Ann, then aged 22, was heavily pregnant with her second child when their wedding took place. The baby, John Thomas, arrived two weeks later. Their first child, Harriet Mary, had been born in March the previous year. After their marriage, Susan's mother Catherine moved into a house on the corner of Elizabeth St and Currie St, and Mary Ann and Henry took over the house next door to Henry Atkin senior. Henry junior, a wood turner by trade like his father, might well have lent a sympathetic ear to Susan after her court case. He had encountered Mr Beddome in the Police Court himself, as a defendant.

Early the following year Susan's sister Margaret married Henry's brother, Thomas Atkin. By the end of 1866 Catherine was grandmother to four grandchildren, three being the children of Mary Ann and Henry Atkins and one the child of Catherine and George Davis. Sadly, Margaret and Thomas Atkins' first and only child, Thomas, died just days after his birth in April 1868.

For Catherine senior these weddings must have brought back memories of her own marriage to John a quarter of a century earlier. Did it bother her that the girls hadn't waited until they were married to produce children, as she and John had done? The Catholic taboo against premarital sex was generally adhered to in Ireland in her younger days. And then there was Susan. She especially was becoming more than Catherine could handle.

Susan and Mr Samuel Beddome came face to face again in December 1867. She and another girl, Susan Cavanagh, were charged with "making use of obscene language" in Currie Street the previous evening. An older woman, Alice Freer, also appeared in court that day for the same offence, committed in Morphett Street.

Almost every week Mr Beddome dealt with similar cases. In keeping with the British law on which their legal systems were based, all the Australian colonies had laws against the use of obscene language. Many of those charged were girls and young women found on the streets at night, and the law seems to have been used as a way of removing them. Mr Beddome fined the girls 10 shillings each, plus court costs of 5 shillings, a total of 15 shillings. Given that serving girls at this time earned about 6 shillings per week, this was quite a hefty fine for what now seems a trivial offence.

Who were these girls? Susan Cavanagh first appeared before Mr Beddome in 1859, when she was arrested for drunkenness and using obscene language. She faced similar charges regularly from then on. Several times she was the victim of assaults, once or twice by another woman, but more often by the mariners who were probably her clients. In August 1863 she was described as "a woman of notorious character". When she assaulted a police officer in June 1867 she was perhaps fortunate only to receive a hefty fine of 40 shillings plus costs. She was sent to prison for 14 days in May 1868 as a common prostitute. In 1869 she was charged with being "a pauper lunatic" but the case was dismissed, on the grounds that she was suffering from delirium tremens, a life-threatening consequence of alcohol withdrawal. Her name disappears from the papers not long after this, perhaps a sad victim of alcohol or physical abuse.

Alice Freer, a slightly older woman, had a similar string of convictions going back to the early 1860s. In 1863 she was charged with assaulting another girl in a dispute over the use of a clothes line. In 1864 she prosecuted a Dr Nott for having withheld £1.8s in wages. She was awarded 12 shillings but made to pay the court costs when it was revealed that she had left his service without notice after carelessly breaking the glass in a picture frame. In 1866 she was openly named as a common prostitute when she was charged with "riotous and indecent behaviour" in Currie Street.

Susan's friend Ann Connor, the witness in the case against Pasquale Nicro, was another frequent attender in the police courts, mostly on charges of using indecent language or petty theft. In May 1865 she was the victim of an attempted rape. Her two assailants, described in the press as "Irish Ruffians", also assaulted the police officer who attempted to help her. They were committed for trial but the outcome is unknown.

Was Susan herself a prostitute? It's possible, even likely, that she was initiated into sexual activity at a young age, willingly or otherwise. She may well have sought comfort in the arms of men. However, she was never arrested for prostitution. Except for Pasquale Nicro, no-one ever publicly called her a whore. Having said that, the company she kept certainly included girls who at some stage were named in court as common prostitutes.

It would hardly be surprising if Susan didn't include some of these girls amongst her friends and acquaintances. Many of them would have grown up together with her in west Adelaide. Entertainment options for girls of her social class were limited. Servant girls didn't get a lot of time to themselves, but when they did, what was there for them to do besides socialise in and around the streets, pubs and dance halls? Someone like Susan, with her lack of education, was unlikely to sit and read a book, embroider doilies or paint watercolours.

Prostitution was rife in the area around Currie Street, Hindley Street and Light Square almost from the time of the first settlement. A few of the prostitutes were girls who had decided they could do better for themselves on the street than by working long hours as a servant for a demanding mistress. Others preferred it to the alternative of facing up to the moral judgement and paternalism of the Destitute Board.

The number of women and girls driven into prostitution by poverty increased rapidly in the 1850's. Between 1848-1850, during the great Irish Famine, several hundred teen-aged orphan girls arrived in South Australia from Irish workhouses under the Earl Grey scheme. Then in 1854 a shortage of servant girls and farm labourers in South Australia led to an influx of single women arriving from Ireland as assisted immigrants, encouraged by the Colonial Land and Immigration

Commissioners who paid their fares. Unfortunately communication between Adelaide and the Commissioners in Britain was slow, and by the time a message got back to London by ship to say "Enough, we don't need any more girls" over 4000 had arrived. To make matters worse, a drought had reduced the demand for farm labourers. South Australia now had a glut of young women looking for work.

Some found work on farms and in country towns, others in Adelaide and surrounding areas, through the employment depots hastily set up by the South Australian authorities or through the Catholic church. Although the girls were described as 'domestic servants' before they arrived, many of them came from rural villages and farms and had no experience as domestic servants.

Because of the girls' poor reputation and their vulnerability, some of the locals felt free to exploit them. They were paid as little as 2s 6d per week plus board, and were expected to work long hours for ungracious employers. Others were unable to find work. Not surprisingly then, although many eventually did well for themselves, a substantial number drifted into prostitution. C W Parkin estimated that 40% of all prostitutes in Adelaide in the 1850s were Irish orphans. Susan, with her Irish Catholic background, would have found it easy enough to make friends with these girls.

The other side of the prostitution equation was the steady stream of men coming in from the bush with their wages, or returning from the gold fields with their profits. They flocked to the pubs and bars, looking for a good time after their lonely and back-breaking work. Once inebriated they could easily be fleeced not just for the cost of having a good time with a girl, but often of any valuables and money they were carrying. Another profitable source of income for Adelaide's west end prostitutes was the soldiers of the British Army regiments stationed in South Australia.

The colony had always had companies of British soldiers present in small numbers. Their presence was not always appreciated, as for instance, in 1847 when some soldiers from the 11th regiment were involved in a drunken riot. South Australia also had its own on-again, off-again militia, the Royal South Australian Volunteer Militia.

From time to time the need for a more substantial force to protect the colony in case of war between Britain and another power such as France was mooted. In 1855, during the Crimean War, fears were frequently expressed that the Russians might try to take one or more of the colonies from Britain, and the home government in London had been asked by the Governor, Sir Henry Young, to send more troops to protect South Australia. At that time, apparently, none could be spared.

But in 1867 the Adelaide newspapers announced that several companies of the 50th regiment, who had recently been fighting in the "Maori Wars" in New Zealand, were to be brought to Adelaide from Taranaki. They were to relieve the men of the 14th regiment who had been in South Australia since November 1866. Not everyone was happy with this. Some, like the editor of the South Australian Register, raised the question of what it would cost the colony to house these men, and more importantly, how were they to be kept occupied?

Nevertheless, when the 232 men and 9 officers of the 50th regiment arrived in Port Adelaide aboard the Hevershem on Saturday 10 August, along with 22 women and 37 children, they were met by a welcoming crowd. From the port they travelled by train (on the rail line built in 1856) to the town and were escorted from the railway station to the barracks by the Volunteer Regimental Band.

Perhaps nineteen year old Susan stood in the crowd that morning, waving to the soldiers as they arrived. She would have been used to seeing British soldiers around the town, in their impractical but impressive scarlet and black uniforms, but she might still have been stirred by this rousing reception.

Was she aware, now that she was old enough to keep a secret, that a company of the 50th regiment had been her father's prison guards on board the Parmelia? Did she hear heated debates in her childhood home about the Fenian rebels' activities, the terrible and unnecessary deaths produced by the Irish potato famine, and Britain's political and military role in Ireland? Did her Irish Catholic background leave her with mixed feelings about British soldiers, despite their fine appearance?

Or was she pragmatic enough to recognise that in reality, many British soldiers spoke with Irish accents. Irish antipathy towards their English overlords did not prevent thousands of them from deciding that it was better to take English sustenance in return for their services as soldiers than to starve with their pride intact. On average, in the mid 19th century nearly 30% of the British army were born in Ireland. Susan's sister Eliza would be courted by one such soldier from the 50th regiment, Jeremiah Murphy, who was born in Cork.

That winter morning in August 1867, Susan could not have known that this troop of red-coats would have a life-changing role in her own story. Perhaps she observed the women accompanying their men that morning, and had a romantic notion of sharing their wandering lifestyle. Was the relationship she developed with one of these soldiers just the result of 'business as usual' for the street-wise Susan, or did she deliberately set out to find herself a husband?

The soldier in question was David Whybrew. David was the son of a farm labourer named James Whybrew and his second wife Sarah, and he was born in the pretty Essex village of Wormingford in 1839. In July 1841 Sarah died and James Whybrew and his family moved to another Essex village, Wakes Colne. James himself died in 1848.

David would have been too young when his father died to find work or care for himself.Apparently no-one in the extended family was able to take him in. His eldest sister Sophia had married, and his other sisters, Harriet and Eliza, were probably working as live-in servants. His older brother Jeremiah, still single, had gone off to North America, where he found work as a carpenter, and later married and raised a family. So David, at the age of ten, became a resident of the Stanway Workhouse, run by the Lexden and Winstree Poor Law Union.

Like the Destitute Asylum in Adelaide, the workhouses of England were intended to be places of last resort for those who could not support themselves in any other way. Although varying in standard, they were generally spartan, cheerless and degrading. Parents were separated from their children, and brothers from sisters. Residents were expected to do whatever work they were capable of doing, no matter how tedious or meaningless it might be.

Yet although life for children in the workhouses was comfortless, it had some benefits. In addition to being clothed and fed, they usually received a basic education. In this sense they were sometimes better off than the children outside the walls of the workhouse who had no schooling. David grew up able to read and write.

By the time he was sixteen he had left the workhouse and after working briefly as a farm labourer he joined the Essex Rifles, a local militia. In December 1856, as soon as he was old enough, he transferred to the 50th (Queen's Own) Regiment as a regular soldier. His enlistment papers state that he was 21 years old, though he was probably barely 18.

Life for the ordinary foot soldier in the British army at this time was essentially a form of slavery. Men could sign up for life or 21 years, but after 21 years without a trade to fall back on, many found re-enlistment the only option. Many of those who became soldiers did so not as a "career choice" but as a way out of poverty, though "stoppages" for rations, clothing and other necessities reduced their daily pay of one shilling to almost nothing. Their status in society was little better than that of criminals. Officers might be invited to balls and swooned over by young ladies, but the lower ranks were welcomed only by prostitutes and beer sellers.

Discipline was harsh. Soldiers could be flogged for losing their tackle or insulting an officer. They could be branded with the letter 'D' (tattooed with permanent ink on their left chest, using a specially manufactured device) or even hanged for desertion. The soldiers who guarded convicts like John Mason and William Doody were not much better off than their captives. And that was in peace time. During a war their lives were often utterly miserable.

Fortunately when David Whybrew enlisted, conditions in the army were slowly beginning to improve. During the

Crimean War, which ended just before David joined up, eye witness accounts of the appalling conditions on and around the battle fields were reported in the British newspapers for the first time, aided by the introduction of the telegraph and photography.

Florence Nightingale was one of those who responded to the reports in a practical way, providing nursing care to the wounded and making drastically needed improvements in the military hospitals of the Crimea. But she was not simply "the Lady of the Lamp". She had money, she had a good education, she had connections in high places, and she used them all to open doors in the British War Office that others said were impenetrable.

She continued to campaign for better conditions for ordinary soldiers long after the Crimean War was over. Proper medical care for sick and wounded soldiers began to be taken seriously, and death rates fell dramatically. The British government also set up a number of enquiries into the running of the army which gradually led to improvements in the lives of the lower ranks over the next 50 years.

David's first posting outside of England was to Ceylon (Sri Lanka) in 1857. His army records show that while he was there he suffered from tropical ulcers and a febrile illness, presumably malaria, which was treated with quinine. He was promoted to Corporal in 1860 and Sergeant in 1863. From Ceylon his company sailed to New Zealand, where they were involved in the Maori Wars of 1863. In 1864 he was demoted back to corporal, for reasons unrecorded, but otherwise he came through his New Zealand experience unscathed.

In 1866 David's company travelled via Norfolk Island, Van Diemen's Land (now Tasmania) and Sydney to

Adelaide, arriving in August 1867. The soldiers were stationed in the barracks near Government House, between North Terrace and the River Torrens. Those with families either shared overcrowded rooms in the barracks, or were housed in dilapidated cottages nearby. The regiment's commanding officer, Colonel Hamley, became the acting Governor of the colony during their stay.

By September 1867 the troops were practising manoeuvres in the North Parklands with members of the local militia, in readiness for the expected arrival on 2 November of Prince Alfred, the Duke of Edinburgh. This royal visit, the first of its kind in South Australia, was a major social event for the small colony and the residents talked about it for weeks before and after it occurred.

The 50th regiment's officers were quickly accepted into the social life of Adelaide's gentry. The ranks found their welcome elsewhere, in the hotels, dance halls and brothels of the city. How Susan and David met, and where, is perhaps best left to the imagination. David, now 30 years old, may well have been thinking that the time had come to find a wife and start a family, but who can tell if he had that in mind when he and Susan began their relationship. What is evident from future events is that it began almost as soon as the regiment arrived in Adelaide.

We have no photos of either of them. David's records indicate that he was of average height and lightly built at 126 lbs (57 kg). His hair, in unimaginative army terms, was brown and his eye colour grey. No description of Susan survives. Given her impoverished childhood she was probably quite short and slender. Perhaps she had her father's grey eyes and brown hair. Or perhaps she inherited the Celtic combination of dark hair, fair skin and blue eyes.

As they got to know each other they would have found they had much in common in their childhood poverty and the experience of losing a parent. Whether this formed a bond between them or made their relationship more difficult as a result of their response to such trauma is something about which we can only speculate.

Where Susan was living at this time - at home with Catherine, boarding at her place of work as a servant girl, or elsewhere - isn't clear, but she gave Elizabeth Street as her address in 1868 when she appeared in the police court with David. This court appearance was to be her longest and most intriguing.

Chapter 6

A girl of such a character – 1868

In the early hours of Saturday, 11 April 1868, just as it was getting light, four revellers made their way back from a hotel in North Adelaide, across the main bridge over the Torrens, towards King William Street. The two men, Corporal David Whybrew and Private Richard Hughes, were wearing the unmistakable red-coated uniforms of the 50th regiment. Their companions were two young women, Bridget Jules and Susan Mason. They had been drinking together since 9 o'clock the previous evening, and were heading back to Susan Mason's house in Elizabeth St.

As they passed the City Baths, they noticed the dark shape of a man lying on the ground and went over to investigate. One of the soldiers shook the sleeping man, a labourer named Frank Jones, and said "You have a hard bed to lie on." Then, as he began to stir, one of the four put a hand in the slumberer's pocket and pulled out a pocket book containing some papers and a watch.

What happened next became the focus of interest when, on the following Tuesday, Bridget Jules and the two soldiers, Whybrew and Hughes, stood in the splendid new Police Courts before Mr Samuel Beddome, charged with "larceny from the person". It fell to Mr Beddome to decide whether there was enough evidence to send the defendants to the Supreme Court, where such cases were usually heard.

But where was Susan Mason? She had somehow become a prosecution witness to the crime rather than a defendant, for reasons we'll see.

As the story unfolded it became clear that the gullible Frank Jones had been robbed more than once that Friday evening. According to his own evidence in court, he had come into the town from Yorke Peninsula and had been drinking at the Shamrock, a hotel in Currie Street. Leaving there, he headed down Hindley Street towards the Albion hotel, where he met two girls (probably not Bridget and Susan), and gave them some money, a few shillings. The newspaper reports left the readers to guess why he might have done this.

After leaving them, he'd found that a money order for one pound was missing from his pocket, so he retraced his steps to the Albion, but the girls, not surprisingly, denied having seen it. He then proceeded up King William Street towards the Baths. Then, feeling tired, he lay down on the steps and fell asleep.

In court he maintained that he was quite sober when he woke and found the two soldiers and the women standing over him. He didn't think the soldiers were drunk. He'd never seen any of the group before, but he had recognised the red uniform of the soldiers. He also claimed to recognise the two women in court. One of them had asked him if he was "going to shout", that is, give them something, and he'd refused.

Then, feeling alarmed, he'd checked his pockets. When he discovered the money order missing from the pocket where it had been, he immediately told them that it would be of no use to them. And then, finding his watch also missing, he'd asked them where it was. One of the soldiers had said "We know nothing of your watch". The four of them had then walked off.

Susan Mason, in her role as a prosecution witness, said that it had been Hughes who rifled through Jones' pockets. He had given all the papers he found, including the money order for £9, to Whybrew, who gave them to her for safekeeping. Whybrew had then put his hand in the man's pockets and removed the watch.

Mr Dempsey, of the Detective Office, called on Detectives Gibbison, Keegan and Doyle for their evidence. The money order had been retrieved, they said, but the watch, worth £6, was still missing. Mr Beddome agreed to their request that the case be remanded until Thursday so that the watch could be found. A surety (or bail) of £25 each was imposed for the two soldiers. Bridget Jules seems to have remained in custody.

On the following Thursday, April 16, the watch had still not been retrieved, but the detectives requested that the case go forward to the Supreme Court, based on the existing evidence. The prisoners were then allowed by Mr Beddome to make a statement if they wished.

David Whybrew's statement is worth quoting verbatim, just as it appeared in the Adelaide Observer on April 18 (formatted slightly to make reading easier).

"On the morning of the 11th of April, between the hours of 3 and 5 o'clock, I and Susan Mason, with Richard Hughes and Bridget Jules, were in company together, and coming from North Adelaide. When we got to the City Baths, we saw a man lying drunk on the steps. Susan

Mason said to Jules, "I will bilk this man," meaning, I suppose, that she would rob him.

She then commenced to search his pockets. After she was satisfied with doing so, the four of us went up the road together. Afterwards Mason and Jules went across the road together away from us. After they had done talking together Mason came back to me and handed me a small account-book. I opened it, and as I did so saw there were only two leaves.

Mason said, "Do not tear that book."

I said, "You have already done that yourself;" saying which I threw the book down, and said I would not have anything to do with the man that was robbed.

She then put her hand into her pocket, saying she thought she had some notes. She showed some papers to me to tell her what they were. It was dark, and I could not tell her what they were with the exception of an order. I could see the figures on that to be £9 1s. 11d.

As soon as I told her the amount she laughed and snatched the order out of my hand, and said in presence of Jules and me that she would get the order cashed in the morning, buy a new dress for herself, and a ring for Jules if she would come to her house for it between 10 and 11.

She put the order and some other papers into her pocket, and said, "I felt some more notes in that man's trousers pocket. I will go back and try again." She did so, and we three went back with her.

When we had got back I saw her put her hand into the man's right-hand trousers pocket and pull out a lot of pieces of paper, some tobacco, and a knife. In doing this a watch fell from the man's pocket on to the step on which he was sitting. I picked the watch up and looked at it. I laid it down again in the same place with the face upwards.

The four of us then proceeded towards Elizabeth Street, and when we got 50 or 60 yards from the spot where the man was robbed Susan Mason said to me, "Give me that little watch, old duck, and I will give you for it one I have at home, which is too big for a woman to carry."

I said to her, "Do you think I was fool enough to take that man's watch?"

She said, "Did you not take it?"

I replied, "No; I laid it down again in the place I took it from." I then, to satisfy her and Jules that I had not got the watch, opened my coat, took my cap off and held it in my hand, and let Mason search me in presence of Jules. They then said they were both satisfied that I had not got the watch.

Mason then said, "You must be a d—d fool not to take the watch."

I replied, "I'd be a bigger fool if I did do so." By this time we had reached Elizabeth Street. There Mason said to Jules, "As soon as those two men go home we will go back again and take the watch and more money if the man has got it."

I separated from Susan Mason and went home to the Barracks. I did not see Mason again until between 11 and 12 o'clock the same morning, when she told me that before she could go out of her own house to get the order cashed, a detective came in and asked her if she had got anything that did not belong to her. To the detective she had given up some papers and the order, saying that she picked them up in King William Street, opposite the Gresham Hotel. She told me to tell the detective the same if he came down to the Barracks to me."

The prisoner Whybrew thenrequested that the Clerk of the Court append thefollowing:

"I am in my twelfth year in the service,and never was charged with either theft or drunkenness since I have been in theservice. I have been six years in India,and between three and four years in thecampaign in New Zealand, doing hard duty,and fighting for my Queen and country whenever required. I now think it very hard if a girl of sucha character is to try and swear her deeds upon myback. That is all I have to say at present."

Hughes then had his much briefer say:

"I know nothing about the transaction. I was stupidly drunk at the time. I am the last man that would do such a thing, and all mycomrades would say the same."

No doubt this account includes some creative editing by the Adelaide Observer's court reporter. It's difficult to know whether the words attributed to Susan in her conversation with David were her own, David's attempted mimicry of her Australian slang, or the reporter's imagination.

Nevertheless, the carefully constructed statement was clearly intended to show David in the best possible light; an almost innocent bystander who had tried to encourage his companions to do the right thing. Both Whybrew and Hughes had lawyers representing them when the case went to the Supreme Court, paid for, presumably, by the army, while poor Bridget Jules went unrepresented. Perhaps David's lawyer, or one of his officers, had helped him to draft this response.

What is remarkable is that it so firmly lays the blame on Susan Mason. Frank Jones, the victim, recognised Susan in court, but he didn't single her out in his evidence. But David paints her as the instigator and main culprit in the crime.

His phrase "a girl of such a character" must have stung. Susan and David had known each other for several months by this time. The statement itself hints that this was no one-night outing. They were evidently quite familiar with each other. What isn't revealed in the newspaper account is that Susan was pregnant at the time with a child that David apparently accepted was his, suggesting that their relationship was by then fairly exclusive.

Yet David wasn't going to sacrifice his career for this girl, or even stand by her. Or perhaps he wasn't going to be allowed to. "Larceny from the person" was a serious offence, carrying a penalty of up to several years imprisonment with hard labour. The British Army would no doubt have had a keen interest in the case. It would not do for two of their soldiers to be found guilty of robbing the very people they were charged with protecting.

But neither was Susan going to stand by David. When the case was heard by Mr Justice Wearing in the Supreme Court one month later, on 19 May, Susan repeated her allegation that it was Hughes who had put his hand in Jones' pocket and removed the papers before handing them to Whybrew. But it was Whybrew, she said, who had taken the watch from Jones' pocket.

This time she added that Jules had also reached into the man's pocket and removed a little bag, and Hughes had wanted to go back and search Jones more thoroughly but had been stopped by Whybrew.

But how did Susan describe her own role in the affair? On Saturday morning, she said, she had gone to Giles and Smith's to look after Jones and deliver back the papers to him. Henry Giles and James Smith ran an import and export business on Waymouth Street and their name appeared on a letter with the money order. After this she had given all the papers to Detective Keegan, perhaps after Giles and Smith refused to cash the order and raised the alarm. She had also gone to the barracks to see David Whybrew and ask him if he had the watch, but he said he'd put it back.

Mr Boucat, David Whybrew's lawyer, asked her what the detectives had said to her. They had told her she wouldn't come to any harm if she told the truth, she said. When asked if she'd had a drink with the detectives on the morning in question, she indignantly replied that she hadn't. And no, she said, she hadn't told Whybrew that he was a fool for not taking the watch.

Questioned by Hughes' lawyer, Mr Stow, she said she hadn't met Hughes before that night, but she had known Whybrew for six months. Both soldiers had been very drunk when they came across Jones, who also seemed drunk, though he had been awake when he was robbed.

Mr Stow repeated Mr Boucat's probing about what the detectives had said to her. She denied that they'd told her that if she gave evidence she wouldn't be prosecuted. Initially, she said, she had told the detectives that she had found the papers near the Gresham.

Detective Keegan, when questioned, said that he had received the papers from Susan Mason, and later in the day David Whybrew had confirmed her false story about finding them near the Gresham. He (Detective Keegan) hadn't arrested her because she had handed him the papers.

It was only later, when he and Detective Gibbison interviewed Whybrew, Hughes and Jules, that he'd discovered that Susan Mason hadn't found the papers in the way she'd described.

When he and the other detectives had interrogated the three prisoners, he said, each had a different version of events. David Whybrew had asked them "if he should get seven years". At this, the two lawyers protested that such evidence ought not to be admitted, but Mr Wearing allowed it to stand.

The two lawyers continued to raise doubts about the way the evidence had been obtained. It would be "monstrously cruel", said Mr Boucat, if the two soldiers were found guilty on the evidence heard that afternoon, and he suggested that if anyone had committed a felony, it was probably Susan Mason. Both Hughes and Whybrew then called on officers from the 50th Regiment, who bore witness to their good characters. Lieutenant. W. L. Fleury spoke on David Whybrew's behalf. Bridget Jules had nothing to say.

Mr Justice Wearing, in summing up, warned the jury not to place much weight on Susan Mason's version of events unless it had been confirmed by the other evidence. The discrepancies between the various stories told by the four, and the reputed good character of the soldiers must also be taken into consideration. The jury took his advice and found the three prisoners "not guilty".

The court case sheds some interesting light on Susan's character, but also raises many questions about her relationship with the other people in the court case and her part in the affair.

Once again we find her in company with a young woman who would later be described in the newspaper's court reports as a common prostitute. Bridget Jules' background is obscure. According to one newspaper she was 22 at the time of the trial, two years older than Susan, and she claimed to have lived in the colony for several years. She was variously described as single, married, or widowed in newspaper reports. Possibly she was one of the Irish girls who arrived in Adelaide in the 1840s and 1850s. She said in court (quite truthfully) that she had never been in any previous trouble, but her name would appear regularly in Police Court reports in the following years, charged with larceny, using obscene language, prostitution and assault.

Whether Susan and Bridget were close friends isn't clear. Susan's offer to buy Bridget a ring (if David's testimony is to be believed) suggests they were close. Yet they happily implicated each other in court, and at one point seem to have got into an argument about the evidence.

Susan's relationship with the detectives also raises questions. Were they genuinely taken in by her handing over the money order and papers to them? She might well have been visibly pregnant at the time of the court case. Did they take pity on her? Or did she, as the lawyer's comments insinuated, have a more familiar relationship with them?

Mr Boucat, in summing up his client Whybrew's case, alluded to "the manner in which Miss Mason had conducted herself in the (witness) box", and pointed out that she was the one who had finished up with "all the plunder". He left the jury in no doubt that Susan was indeed a woman of dubious character and her evidence should not be relied upon to convict his client. But was this a fair assessment of her part in the story?

The army's lawyers clearly thought it in their clients' best interests to paint Susan as the chief villain. She was portrayed as an experienced thief who had used her womanly wiles not only to drag Whybrew and Hughes into taking part in a crime, but also to hoodwink the detectives investigating the case. In contrast, their clients were loyal servants of the Queen with no past record of crime, and they had stupidly fallen in with her illicit activities while inebriated. Her blunt speech and assertiveness in court were not qualities admired in a woman in that era, and the jury may well have agreed with the lawyers' assessment of her.

No doubt Susan was streetwise enough to know how to relieve a drunk of the contents of his pockets. Her reported willingness to lie about her own part in the crime, and to leave her companions in trouble, is not to her credit. Perhaps she really was the chief villain.

Yet there is something rather naive, almost touching, about Susan's response to finding herself in possession of the money order. Her glee at this windfall is child-like. Nine pounds was more than six months wages for a servant girl. It's unlikely that she often saw that amount of money in one place.

In her imagination she already saw the new dress she would buy for herself from the drapers in Rundle St, the ring she would buy for her friend. She'd swap the watch she had (from another theft, maybe) for one that was more her size. She didn't say it, but perhaps she reasoned that Frank Jones would probably only drink the money away anyway. He hadn't come to any harm from his experience of being robbed.

For a couple who were supposedly going out together, there seemed to be little love or loyalty between David and Susan. Yet the discrepancies in their stories helped to bring about a dismissal of the case. Were they perhaps working together to produce such a result? Or did the lawyers' skills pitted against Susan's wiliness produce a stalemate? Overall, the case certainly went the way the army would have liked. Whatever the truth, this was not the end of David and Susan's relationship.

Chapter 7

Motherhood and marriage – 1868-1870

Four months after the court case, on 17 September, Susan's first child Harriet was born. Perhaps she was named after David's sister Harriet, whom he hadn't seen since joining the army twelve years earlier. Or perhaps Susan was fond of her little niece, Harriet Atkin. It's likely that she gave birth at home, with a family member or friend acting as midwife. Births in hospital were unusual, and only the most desperate went to the lying-in ward of the Destitute Asylum to give birth. Stories circulated of destitute women choosing to give birth in hen sheds and under trees rather than go there.

Giving birth to a child, particularly a first child, was a painful, exhausting and potentially life threatening process in 1868. Susan may well have been quite malnourished and small boned as a result of her childhood, making labour more difficult. Queen Victoria's chloroform-assisted delivery in 1853 had helped set a new trend in pain relief during childbirth, but it's unlikely this would have been available to Susan, as chloroform required a doctor to administer it. Opium or brandy were more freely available for pain relief.

Was Susan given time to hold her baby after it was born or was it whisked away while she was recovering from her ordeal? It was common, though not universal, at this time for children born to single mothers to be removed from them at birth and fostered out, either privately to relatives or friends, or to a suitable family appointed through the Destitute Board. Single women were considered morally unsuitable to be parents of a young child. Only in 1868 did the Catholic Church in Adelaide set up a refuge in Franklin Street for single mothers and their children. Susan was not among its inmates.

Susan herself may have decided that it was better for Harriet if she were fostered by someone else. By law, fathers in South Australia were expected to provide for their own children, even those who were illegitimate (ie born outside of marriage), and they could be sued for failing to do so. However, given David's occupation, with its meagre pay and unpredictable relocations, Susan could not rely upon his support to raise Harriet. As early as May 1868 the officers of the 50th regiment had been told to prepare for the order to leave Adelaide. Susan could not work and look after a baby at the same time, and being a single mother would make finding work more difficult, so the risk was high that both she and Harriet would become destitute.

Fortunately for Harriet, the practice of "baby farming", whereby mothers of illegitimate infants paid someone else to take their child and care for it, had not yet become common in South Australia. Horrifying reports of the deaths of many of these infants from malnutrition, unexplained injuries or neglect started appearing in the Adelaide newspapers in the early 1870s and continued into the next century.

If Susan didn't look after Harriet herself, who did? According to some of her living descendants, Harriet Whybrew was brought up by the Lindrum family in

Adelaide. They recall Walter Lindrum, the great billiards player, visiting Harriet in England in later life to pay his respects.

Walter's grandfather, Frederick Wilhelm Lindrum, migrated to South Australia from Germany, and was the landlord of the Clarence Hotel in King William Street in Adelaide. He ran a popular billiards room, frequented by the officers of the 50th regiment. In 1862 he married another German migrant, Clara Wolff, in Adelaide.

At the time of Harriet Whybrew's birth the Lindrums had a 3 year old son, Frederick William, and Clara was heavily pregnant with her second child. She gave birth to a girl, also named Clara, on 2 October. With Frederick weaned and another child on the way, it seems debatable that they would have taken in Harriet from birth, though they may have taken on her care later. No record of Harriet being handed over to the Lindrums survives in the minutes of the Destitute Board, which handled any formal transfer of children.

Another possibility is that Susan's sister Mary Ann and her husband Harry Atkin took in Harriet initially and she became known to the Lindrum family through them. When Harriet Whybrew was born, Mary Ann had only recently lost her six week old son, Sydney, and may have welcomed having another baby to care for. The Atkin's eldest daughter Harriet Mary went on to marry the younger Frederick Lindrum in 1886.

Whatever the case, only a few months after Harriet's birth Susan and David faced a crisis. In December the army announced that the 50th Regiment would be sailing from the colony in early April 1869 and returning to England. The choice was stark. They could either marry or separate. If they separated they would be unlikely to see each other again, and Susan would be left as a "fallen woman". If they married, Susan would have to leave her family and follow David wherever the army took him. It was a difficult decision to make, and they apparently delayed making it for several months.

As mentioned previously, Susan's older sister Eliza had been going out with another soldier of the 50th regiment, Jeremiah Murphy. They married in March 1869, not long before the regiment began its exit from South Australia. Eliza sailed with Jeremiah on the troop ship Himalaya. What might have prevented David and Susan from doing the same?

Perhaps, unlike Jeremiah, David was unable to gain permission from the army to marry. Wives were seen as a mixed blessing by the army hierarchy. They provided a ready source of cooks, launderers and cleaners, and kept the men out of the brothels. At the same time some officers thought that the women and their children were an encumbrance that distracted the men from their duties and made manoeuvring more difficult. It was British army policy to allow only a small percentage of its troops to be married - one in twelve in a garrison such as South Australia.

To gain permission from the army to marry, a man had to have served for at least 7 years (which David had) and be of good character (which was technically true). His prospective wife also had to be of impeccable moral standards (which in Susan's case was disputable). Fathering an illegitimate child was not considered an adequate reason to be given permission to marry.

That didn't mean that men couldn't legally marry without the army's permission, and many men did. But if they married without the consent of the army, their wives and children could not live with them in the barracks, or receive rations from the army. Their wives would have to support themselves and their children, and they would not be included in any travel arrangements. They would not be "on the strength" and their existence would be ignored by the army.

Susan may have been reluctant to marry David while he remained in the army. She had known him for nearly two years and had plenty of time to observe the life led by the wives of other soldiers of the regiment. Perhaps to a strong-willed, independent woman like Susan, used to making her own decisions and going where she pleased, such an ordered, restricted life didn't appeal. The prospect of living as a wife "off the strength" must have been even less appealing.

The thought of being separated from her mother, sisters, nieces and nephews, friends and familiar faces may also have held her back. She had spent her whole life in Adelaide. Could she even imagine life elsewhere? Almost everyone in Adelaide except the local Kaurna people had arrived from somewhere else, but most expected to remain there for the rest of their lives. Travelling in order to see the world wasn't the norm, even for young people, and especially not for young women.

And she was a mother now. While she remained in Adelaide she could see little Harriet, even if she wasn't able to care for her. But if she sailed for England she might never see her child again. That, surely, was motivation enough to stay.

However, she must have been under considerable pressure to marry from her family and community. In Adelaide, the "City of Churches", premarital sex was frowned upon, though it was not uncommon for couples to anticipate their marriage and give birth to their first child less than 9 months after the wedding. Some, like her older sister Mary Ann, anticipated the wedding more than once. But in general, the only girls who gave birth while still unmarried were those who had the misfortune to become pregnant to married men, or to men from a much higher social class who refused to marry beneath them. To be left behind as a single mother would condemn Susan to being a social outcast.

If David did apply for permission to marry Susan, no record of the request exists in his army papers. Perhaps he knew what the answer would be. On the other hand, if David had wanted to end the relationship with Susan, he would have had the perfect opportunity to do so with the departure of his regiment. He could have marched from the barracks to the railway station, wiping a tear from his eye as the local militia band played "Auld Lang Syne" and "The Girl I Left Behind Me", and joined his mates on the Himalaya, which was docked in Port Adelaide. That would have been the end of it.

Instead, David chose to go into hiding when the Himalaya sailed on 1 April. His name appeared in the South Australian Police Gazette on 28 April as a deserter from his regiment and he became a hunted man.

Desertion from the army was not uncommon. According to one newspaper report, up to 40 soldiers deserted the 50th regiment while it was stationed in South Australia. However, it was a serious offence. In the same report, one soldier from the 50th Regiment found guilty of desertion was sentenced to 2 years imprisonment, while another received 66 days in prison, both with hard labour. David took a considerable risk in staying behind when his ship sailed.

Given the possible consequences, which he would have been well aware of in advance, David must have had strong reasons for staying in Adelaide. Had he decided at the last moment that he couldn't leave Susan? He was nearly thirty years old, their relationship was long-standing though not without its complexities. Perhaps he had begun to feel that it was time to settle down and establish a family.

Did he perhaps hope to leave the army altogether, laying low for a while before assuming the life of a South Australian citizen? He had no strong ties to family in England. He could make a new life in the colony, where labourers and other unskilled workers were in demand. Many soldiers did this successfully.

Whatever the case, he seems to have had second thoughts about his decision. On 19 May, after seven weeks in hiding, David and another soldier named John Love gave themselves up to the police. Where he had been and what contact he had with Susan while he was in hiding is unrecorded. Susan fell pregnant again some time between the end of March and the beginning of May. Perhaps news of the pregnancy had something to do with David's reappearance.

Just a few days later, on Friday 28 May, they were married at St Luke's Church of England on Whitmore Square. It must have been a brief and quiet affair. Susan's mother Catherine, if she was there, would no doubt have had mixed feelings about her wayward daughter marrying an English soldier. Susan's closest sister, Eliza, had already left for England, but her oldest sister Mary Ann and her brother-in-law Thomas Atkin, Margaret's husband, were there to serve as witnesses. David signed the register with his full name but Susan signed with an 'X'.

David was still under arrest, so it's likely that either the police or an army guard also attended the wedding. Given David's circumstances, the army must have played some role in the wedding arrangements, whether simply by giving consent for him to leave detention for a few hours, or by actively encouraging him to do the deed.

On 5 June David and John Love appeared in the Adelaide Police Court before Mr Beddome. They pleaded 'not guilty' to the charge of desertion, agreeing instead to sign a declaration that they were 'absent without leave'. What penalty Mr Beddome imposed is not mentioned in the newspaper report. In most such cases the guilty parties were handed over to the military to deal with.

The following two years may well have been a period in which Susan and David were separated for much of the time. It's probable that David would have served at least some time in a military prison, either in Adelaide or on his return to England. He must have left Adelaide by early May 1870, since he was with his regiment in Bristol, England by 29 June 1870. Three months later, perhaps at the end of his detention, he was demoted from corporal back to private. It was a dismal start to David and Susan's married life.

No record survives of Susan's journey or her arrival in England. Did she travel with David, or make her own way to England? Did the army pay for her travel, or did she raise the fare of about £20 herself? It's clear that she remained in Adelaide at least until their daughter Eliza was born, since Eliza's birth on 10 December 1869 was registered in South Australia. Susan's name next appears in the public records sixteen months later in the UK census in April 1871, when she was living in Aldershot in Hampshire. David moved with his regiment from Bristol to the camp in Aldershot in March that year. Their third child was not conceived until at least early April, raising the possibility that she and David had been separated before this.

Whether Susan travelled to England with David or alone, the two-month voyage in a cramped ship was to be a one way journey. We can only imagine what thoughts went through her mind as she clutched Eliza close to her and watched the Adelaide plain and the tree-covered slopes of the Mount Lofty ranges recede into a grey blur in the distance. She must have heard stories from her parents about the long sea voyages they had endured. Now she was repeating their journeys in reverse, leaving behind, as they had done, almost everything and everyone she knew.

As a married woman with a child, her status in the world she was leaving had briefly risen several notches above what it had been as a single mother and companion of the girls on the streets. But now she was an army wife, "off the strength" and therefore practically non-existent to the British army. Soldiers of David's rank had no social respectability to share with their spouses. How would she fare in the world she was entering as an illiterate 21 year old?

Chapter 8

The army wife – 1870-1885

Conditions for passengers on board ship had improved considerably since her father John's journey in 1833, due in part to the requirements of free settlers travelling to Australia, but they were still not salubrious. For those who could afford the cost of a cabin on an upper deck, the journey was uncomfortable but bearable. For someone like Susan, a passage to England meant sharing a damp, poorly lit berth in steerage with little privacy.

In the tropics the heat in the lower decks was stifling, particularly if a storm necessitated closing the hatches. The stench of the communal privies, mixed with the pungent smell of the chloride of lime used to disinfect the decks, was unavoidable, as were the rats, fleas, lice and other vermin. Susan, used to living with a large family, would perhaps have found the overcrowding and lack of privacy less of a problem than the sense of confinement.

Caring for a young baby without mother or older sisters to help must have been a test of Susan's skills, as well as intensifying her sense of separation. Perhaps she found a more experienced mother on board to give her advice and support in looking after Eliza. Despite the risks and difficulties of ship-board life, she and Eliza both arrived safely at their destination.

Which port provided her first view of England? No record exists. Wherever it was, Susan would have found that this place that the South Australian newspapers always referred to as "Home", was not very home-like at all. The English countryside was softer and greener than the South Australian bush, while the streets of the cities and towns were cramped and grey and convoluted compared to wide straight streets of Adelaide. She would have missed having the clear expanse of the sky above her. At night the dense arc of the Milky Way, seen so clearly in Adelaide, was barely visible in the English sky.

The English people around her might wear the same clothes, speak the same language and live under the same legal system as in South Australia, but they were subtly different from the people she had grown up with. The English class system was more complex and long-established, and it would have taken her a while to find her place in it. No doubt her accent was a constant source of curiosity to people used to summing up another's context from their way of speaking. Her Australian colloquialisms were probably sometimes misunderstood. Even her expletives weren't always recognised.

The wages of a foot soldier such as David were intended only to keep himself well-fed enough to do his duty, not to feed and house a family, and Susan needed to find work as soon as possible to support herself and little Eliza. But she had no references, no-one to commend her, no real experience. David was expected to fulfil his commitments to the army, which meant that he was more an irregular visitor than a companion in her life. Everything she did she had to work out for herself.

She found accommodation in Aldershot with a couple named Henry and Charlotte Hudson and began work as a general servant, probably with the Hudsons themselves. Henry Hudson had served with David in the 50th regiment in Ceylon and New Zealand but he was now an army pensioner, as a result of a hernia which rendered him unable to perform normal duties. He was discharged from the army completely in 1874.

The Hudson's house in Redan Gardens was a couple of miles, or a half hour's walk, away from the barracks in South Camp, where David lived. The barracks was also home to Susan's sister Eliza and her husband Jeremiah. Several of the other soldiers' wives at the barracks came from South Australia and may have been known to Susan, but whether they included her in their social circle is uncertain.

Eliza Murphy's life was quite different to Susan's, though not necessarily preferable. Eliza was "on the strength". She and her infant daughter Maria lived with Jeremiah, and received rations from the army. The army also provided schooling for older children in the camp. But while the army recognised the usefulness of women in the barracks, and paid them a pittance for their services as nurses, washerwomen and seamstresses, their interest in the wives' welfare didn't go much further than that. The accommodation provided for a family might be a separate room, but it could be just a section of the barracks screened off by blankets. Women in these circumstances had to eat, sleep, even give birth, within ear shot of the other men.

Soldiers wives were also subject to army discipline, including having their living quarters inspected daily. On Sundays they were expected to go to church. One wife complained that her husband's commanding officer even expected her to salute him when she met him in the street. When their husbands were sent overseas, wives were not guaranteed either a passage with him or accommodation while he was away, which meant they could be left at the mercy of the civilian Poor Law authorities for support. Only after 1873, under the Cardwell reforms, were soldiers expected by law to maintain their families, and this applied only to those "on the strength" and was not widely enforced.

While marriage was discouraged among the lower ranks, the upper ranks of the army were free, even expected, to marry. Officers' wives often acted as an informal welfare system, visiting the sick, providing gifts at Christmas and giving philanthropic support to soldiers' families in distress. On the other hand, if they chose to, they could also make the lives of the lower ranking wives quite miserable.

As they acclimatized to the English weather and way of life, Susan and her sister Eliza both added to their families. Eliza and Jeremiah's second child, James, arrived in 1871. Then in early 1872 Susan gave birth to a boy, proudly naming him David. David senior might have wondered if his son would follow him into the army. For Susan there was perhaps the bittersweet realisation that while this child gave her an anchor in England, her family in Australia would probably never meet him.

Eliza gave birth to Roseanna in 1873, and Susan followed suit with Rosina early in June 1874. By then, both families had moved from Aldershot to the garrison town of Colchester in Essex. For Eliza and Jeremiah, this meant moving themselves, their children and their few possessions to new barracks. They had little choice in where they lived, but at least they knew in advance from other army couples whether their accommodation would be better or worse than the ageing wooden huts in Aldershot. For Susan it meant packing up and finding employment and new accommodation for herself and her two children in a place that was totally unknown to her.

Colchester was home ground for David. It had been the nearest large town when he was growing up in Wormingford, and he had probably visited the markets or been there on other special occasions. His much older half-sister Louisa Springett, recently widowed, lived in Barrack Street in Colchester, and three of his other sisters, Sophia Duncombe, Eliza Moss and Harriet Hubbard, lived with their families within ten kilometres of the town. Nothing is known of what interaction Susan and her children had with David's family.

Colchester had been a military town from Roman times, and the evidence of that military presence was everywhere, from the impressive ruins of the castle on its mound in the centre of the town, to the barracks, parade grounds and new army housing scattered around it. The town's other main industry, perhaps not unconnected, was beer brewing. David, naturally, took up residence in the barracks, while Susan seems to have found accommodation on nearby Golden Hill (now Golden Noble Hill).

Without telephone, or even telegraph, the only way for Susan and her sister Eliza to share news with family back in Australia was by letter, sent by sea. Susan was illiterate, but she might have asked someone else to write for her. If the families did exchange letters, the sad news of their mother Catherine's death in March 1874 would have reached Susan and Eliza about the time that Susan and David's daughter Rosina was born.

Susan must have felt a long way from home. But soon she would have her sad news of her own to share with her family. In March, three months before Rosina was born, David senior had contracted measles. It's surprising that a man of 35, who had spent so much time in institutions of various kinds, had not had measles earlier in his life, but the army doctor confirmed the diagnosis. If David had measles, it's likely that so did his children. Susan would have had her hands full nursing them while trying to keep them fed and clothed.

Fortunately David senior recovered from his infection without any ill effects. But on 18 July 1874, only six weeks after Rosina's birth, little David died after a week-long struggle with pneumonia. Mary Burke - a nurse perhaps, or a neighbour - who was present at his death signed the death certificate. He was buried in the cemetery in Colchester not long after his second birthday. For Susan, his loss must have revived memories of being separated from Harriet, and no doubt made her more anxious for the safety of her new baby.

Then, while Susan was still grieving her son's death, and recovering from Rosina's birth, David informed her that the army was moving the 50th regiment to Dublin in Ireland.

The British Government maintained a military presence in Ireland to remind the population of who was in control. Many different regiments rotated through the various Irish barracks, which stretched across the country from Belfast in the north east to Kinsale on the south coast.

The army's presence was mostly unnecessary in what was then a fairly quiet time in Ireland's history. The Fenians, who sought home rule through violent uprising, still existed, but after the Catholic church outlawed them in 1870 they were much less active than they had been. The battle for Home Rule was focused, for now, on increasing the number of Irish members in the British parliament, in an effort to bring about reform through legislation.

Susan was faced with staying alone in Colchester with her two girls, or finding some way of going with David to Ireland. Her sister Eliza Murphy, heavily pregnant, would be travelling with Jeremiah. Perhaps it was the prospect of having no dependable financial support except what she could earn herself, and a need to stay close to David and her sister in her grief, that made Susan decide she should go with him. Curiosity to see the country where her parents had been born might also have played a part in her decision.

But as an "off the strength" army wife, she had no automatic right to travel with the troops. Even wives who were "on the strength" sometimes faced a ballot for places when their husbands were posted overseas. How she succeeded in getting to Ireland is something of a mystery.

Perhaps she was able to get a place with the regiment from another woman who had chosen not to go, as sometimes happened. Or possibly she or David managed to persuade his officers to take pity on her. David's commanding officer was still Captain William Fleury, who had provided David's character reference in court in 1868. He and David were about the same age. Like David, Captain Fleury had married while the regiment was stationed in South Australia, and he and his wife Mary had a young family. He may have been sympathetic to the Whybrews' plight. Whatever the case, Susan somehow managed to get herself and her children to Dublin, whether with the men on the troop ship Simoom or on a civilian vessel.

The voyage across the Irish Sea could be rough and unnerving, but it was blessedly brief compared to the journey from Australia. When the regiment arrived in Dublin on 8 August the men were housed in the Ship Street barracks, on the south side of imposing Dublin Castle. Newspaper reports of their arrival say nothing about where the families were housed. Wives were not always housed with their spouses during their time in Ireland. However, it appears from later evidence that Susan was able to live in the barracks with David, at least initially.

Dublin served as a major administrative centre for the British presence in Ireland, and the Lord Lieutenant, the Queen's viceroy, had his residence there. Did Susan feel at home on the Dublin streets, hearing the familiar sound of Irish voices around her, or were they drowned out by the various English accents of the army and government officers on every side? Did she feel any sense of irony in returning to her parents' home country as the wife of a British soldier?

Her surroundings would soon have been far from her mind. Shortly after they arrived in Dublin the baby, Rosina, became ill with a diarrhoeal infection. It was a common illness among infants, especially those living in crowded conditions, and was a frequent cause of death. Susan's anxiety would have increased in intensity day by day as, despite everything she tried, the diarrhoea persisted and Rosina continued to lose weight. Over the next couple of weeks the child stopped feeding and became emaciated and listless. On 18 October, at the age of four and a half months, she died.

David was present at her death in the barracks, and it was he who completed the details for her death registration. Did this second tragedy within four months bring he and Susan together, or did it drive a wedge of resentment between them? The Ship Street Barracks, which would one day become a prison for women involved in the uprising of 1916, would surely have seemed a grim and detestable place to Susan. If ever she loved the army life, it wasn't now.

Eliza Murphy, who had given birth to a son just a few weeks earlier, no doubt did what she could to comfort her sister. But as Susan stood beside another little grave, listening to the funeral rites being read, she must have wondered what had she done, that for the third time a child had been taken from her. Did she blame herself, or her circumstances? Did she still have faith enough to pray, or even just to shake her fist at heaven?

Eight months after Rosina's death an event occurred that must have brought back childhood memories for Susan. Some time before midnight on 18 June 1875 a fire broke out in Malone's Excise Bonded Stores in Ardee Street, not far from the Castle. Many of the 1800 puncheons of whiskey stored there exploded, sending burning rivers of liquid through the streets. The fire brigade were unable to use water to put out the flames, and struggled for many hours to bring the fire under control. In the end they resorted to breaking up the paving and using sand and even animal manure to smother the fire. Men from the 2nd and 50th regiments were called out of their barracks to help fight the blaze, which destroyed 35 buildings, and left many people homeless.

Dublin was to remain the regiment's base until the following autumn, when those troops who had not already been moved to Birr (formerly Parsonstown in County Offaly, or Kings County) were transferred there. Companies from the regiment were rotated through the training grounds on the wide grassy plains at Curragh, south west of Dublin, to practice their musketry. They had little else to do. Only the members of the regimental band were kept busy during their stay in Ireland, called upon regularly to play for social gatherings, balls, sporting events and concerts. The rest of the troops spent their time practising their drills and doing guard duty, without ever seeing any action.

Perhaps David found himself with more time to spend with Susan. Neither grief nor frustration over the lack of a place to call home affected Susan's fertility and by Christmas 1874 she was pregnant again. The birth of their daughter Alice was registered in Birr on 10 September 1875.

The unsettling relocations continued. In August 1876 David's company was moved to Kinsale, in County Cork, and then in March 1877 to Bantry on the west coast. When most of the regiment sailed from Queenstown, Co. Cork in April 1878 for their next posting in Edinburgh, Jeremiah Murphy went too, taking Eliza and the children along. He left the army in December that year and the family settled in Scotland. But Susan and David did not go to Edinburgh with them.

They had already said goodbye to Eliza and Jeremiah several months before this. David left the 50th regiment not long after he had been promoted to sergeant in September 1877, to take up a post as a permanent staff sergeant with the 3rd Battalion of the East Kent Militia, a reserve battalion stationed in Canterbury, Kent. Though Susan and Eliza may not have realised it at the time, their farewell meeting before Susan's departure from Ireland was probably the last time the two sisters would see each other.

David and Susan and the children would most likely have sailed from Queenstown to a port somewhere in the south of England. As they left the Queenstown harbour, formerly known as Cobh, Susan would have had a view out across the waters around Spike Island, to where her father had once been incarcerated on board the prison hulk Surprise. The hulk was long gone, sold and broken up, but the fortress-like prison on Spike Island still stood there. Though she may not have been aware of the significance of what she was seeing that autumn morning, this was the final stage in her long journey back to her roots.

What made David decide to leave the regular army at the age of 40 and join the staff of the militia? The most likely explanation is that he had completed his twenty one year contract with the 50th regiment and took the opportunity to take up a more settled existence. Changes made to army regulations in the early 1870s allowed men to enlist for as little as six years at a time, and to re-enlist for periods of five years. The intention was to encourage men to postpone getting married until they had completed their contract, but the changes also benefited those who were already married. David signed on as a staff sergeant for five years.

Susan may well have had an influence on David's decision not to re-enlist in the regular army. She too must have been weary of the frequent moves that the army forced upon them.

Now nearly thirty, and having given birth five times, Susan arrived in Canterbury with two children, 9 year old Eliza and 3 year old Alice. Initially, it seems, she lived close to the barracks in Northgate. Once again she had the task of re-establishing herself and her household.

This time her sister Eliza was far away in Edinburgh and Susan may not have known any of the other army wives in the Canterbury barracks. Nor did her sharp tongue help her to make friends. In August 1879, while pregnant again, she got into an argument with a neighbour, Bridget Lyon, and appeared in the local magistrates court charged with using obscene language. The judge dismissed the charge, saying that both women seemed as bad as each other.

Then in July 1880 an altercation between Susan and the family of a man named James Foggarty outside the barracks resulted in Foggarty assaulting David when he came to Susan's assistance. Foggarty, despite his argument that he was provoked, received a fine of 5s plus costs when the matter came to court.

Perhaps such frictions left Susan unhappy with living in Canterbury. When the census was taken a few months later in April 1881, David was in the barracks in Canterbury, but Susan and the children were 31 kilometres (19 miles) away in Dover, in a house in Bulwark Lane close to the port. The fact that she is described as the head of the household, with no other occupants besides her family, suggests this was her regular accommodation, not just a place she was visiting. Her occupation is listed simply as "wife of Sergeant Wibram (sic), EK militia". Possibly David divided his time between the barracks and Dover, depending on where the army needed his services most.

News from Australia, if she received any, would often have been dispiriting. Susan's sister Rose Morris died in May 1878 at the age of 31. She and her husband William Morris had moved to Lambton in New South Wales, and it took two weeks for a death notice to appear in the Adelaide newspapers. It's unlikely that Susan heard the news until many months after that, if at all.

The following year, 1879, may have brought news of the death of another sister, Margaret. Susan's younger sister Jane, still single, was admitted to hospital about the same time. Jane appears to have died from cirrhosis in February 1886 at the age of 33. But a trickle of good news coming from Australia and Scotland may also have reached Susan, with her sisters Mary Ann, Catherine and Eliza adding new children to their families on a regular basis.

Susan seems to have been more fortunate in her own childbearing during her seven years in Kent. Daughter Rose was born soon after their arrival in Canterbury from Ireland at the end of 1877. Benjamin John (known as John or Jack) was born towards the end of 1879 and David Henry (known as Henry) in the spring of 1882. Their births were all registered in Canterbury, so possibly Susan's stay in Dover was brief.

The whole family, including David, moved to 17 Berry Street in Sittingbourne, on the other side of Canterbury, after Henry's birth and William (Bill) was born in there in October 1884. The four children born in

Kent all survived infancy and Susan would have been kept busy caring for them while being constantly pregnant or breastfeeding. Her daughter Eliza, now in her teens, would no doubt have been called on to help look after the younger children. Whether Susan was able to do anything to supplement her income, or relied solely on David's meagre salary during this time, is unknown.

Then in 1885, it seems, the family went through some sort of crisis. In August that year, for reasons not recorded, David requested that he be discharged from the East Kent militia, even though he was only two years into a five year contract. His request was granted. The Whybrews subsequently moved back to Colchester in Essex, which they had left over ten years previously.

Their next child, Alfred, was born in Colchester late in 1888. The four year gap between the births of William and Alfred is unusual, breaking the pattern of a birth every two years. Was Susan or David unwell? Were they experiencing increasing strains in their relationship?

If Susan had been of a superstitious nature, events in Sittingbourne in May 1885 might well have made her anxious to leave that area. Workmen digging foundations for a cottage not far from their home in Sittingbourne discovered eighteen skulls and other bones on the site. The bones' size and strength, and the absence of any coffins, suggested that they belonged to ancient Saxons who had died in a bloody battle. The same short column of the local paper which described this find on 23 May also reported that a small boy had recently been attacked by a performing monkey while he and other children were watching its antics. The monkey's owner was an itinerant Italian musician. And then in the same newspaper column came the report of a Coroner's enquiry into the death of another young boy in Sittingbourne, apparently as a result of being beaten by his school master. The boy's surname was Mason.

Even if Susan did not read these disturbing reports, she would surely have heard them discussed by her neighbours. But the Whybrews' life was to be shaken by a development much closer to home, perhaps one that became the trigger for their crisis. Sometime between 1885 and 1888 their first-born child Harriet, left behind in South Australia as an infant, re-entered their lives. It was not to be a very happy or successful reunion.

Chapter 9

Reunion and conflict – 1885-1890

We must now go back to where we left Harriet in 1870, apparently in the care of the Lindrum family in Adelaide. Frederick Lindrum was not only the landlord of the Clarence Hotel with its billiard saloon in King William Street, but also the owner of several other properties in South Australia. When he died in February 1880, his obituary described him as a well respected man with a large circle of friends.

Even before Frederick's death his wife, Clara, became known for her propensity to spend more than they could afford. It seems that she proved unable to effectively manage the properties which she inherited. Within a few months of Frederick's death she advertised the Crown Hotel in Port Victor for sale, and in May 1881 she advertised the sale of household goods and furniture from her properties in Adelaide, before moving to the hotel in Ardossan, 150 km from the city.

By the end of 1881 she had begun making appearances in the Adelaide Insolvency Court, and in December she was declared insolvent. She then disappeared without trace from public life. Her name was not mentioned in newspaper notices when her daughter Clara married in Adelaide in 1885, nor when Frederick junior married Harriet Atkin (Harriet Whybrew's cousin) in Melbourne in 1886. There is no known record of her death or remarriage.

Harriet Whybrew would have just turned 13 years old at the time that Mrs Clara Lindrum disappeared. If she did indeed spend her childhood in the care of the Lindrums, they were no longer her guardians at this stage of her life. It seems likely that her legal guardianship passed to her aunt, Susan's sister, Mary Ann Atkins.

Harriet had reached an age where she was old enough to go out to work and she apparently found employment as a 'nurse girl', a term used for a young girl employed as a child minder or nanny. But this did not last long. In January 1882 she was charged with stealing a watch and various other articles from Frances Sophia Harris, the daughter of John Harris, who owned a general goods cum second hand shop in Rosina Street in Adelaide. One account said Harriet was living with Francis Harris at the time.

She found herself in court, as her mother had done years ago, before Mr Samuel Beddome. Mr Beddome was now a wealthy man as a result of his investments in mining stocks, but he continued to preside over the Adelaide Police Court, with no plans to retire. If he recognised Harriet's surname or noted any similarities between her and her mother Susan, he said nothing. Harriet admitted to having pawned all the articles, except the watch, with a Mr Berliner. Mr Beddome sentenced her to a year in the Industrial School in Magill.

The sentence must have made her heart sink. The Industrial School, located in Adelaide's foothills, was managed by the Destitute Board. "Wayward children" and orphans awaiting placement were sent there to be taught useful skills as well as training them to become "virtuous, honest and useful citizens". Children convicted by the courts were sent to the boys' or girls' reformatories attached to the school to serve their sentences. Despite the skills they acquired, a record of having spent time there made it very difficult for girls to find work afterwards, as it was taken to be a sign of bad character.

The entry in the Destitute Persons record book for Harriet's admission to the Female Reformatory School gives her address as Elizabeth Street, Adelaide. It states that she had parents in England, and an "uncle, David Whybrew, turner, Adelaide". It seems that the writer had confused her father's name with that of her uncle, Henry Atkins, who was indeed a wood turner. Henry and her aunt Mary Ann lived in Elizabeth Street.

Harriet was admitted to the school on 17 January 1882. At the time she was said to be 15 years old, although she was actually not yet 14. By 3 May she was in court before Mr Beddome again, along with several other girls from the school, charged with "riotous behaviour and destroying government property".

The girls had evidently refused to come inside from the garden when asked by the matron, and had threatened to break the laundry windows with stones. While the matron was seeking help from the gardener to get them back inside, they had made a rush for the door and barricaded themselves in the kitchen, where they proceeded to smash crockery and windows and turn the furniture upside down. When it looked as though they were about to make their escape the matron telegraphed for troopers to come and help her.

In court the girls showed an apparent lack of remorse, laughing and treating the whole thing as a huge joke, at least according to the reporter from the South Australian

Weekly Chronicle. Unamused, Mr Beddome sentenced the giddy girls to two months in prison with hard labour. For women and girls, hard labour meant working in the prison laundry, washing sheets and uniforms.

Harriet returned to finish her time at the school in Magill on 1 July. That, however, was not the end of the matter. Having spent time in prison together, the group of girls were now united in their dislike of Matron McColl, and they soon made their dislike clear. On 16 October they were back in court on a further charge of damaging property at the Reformatory School. Dr Mann, the visiting doctor at the school, reported that when he visited the school the previous week, he could see evidence of "a general revolution among the inmates" and the Matron told him that she felt "in fear of her life".

Dr Mann had decided to call the police. A violent struggle had resulted, with objects being thrown and windows broken, when the police arrived and attempted to put the girls in straight jackets. (These were apparently available at the school for just such occasions.) Eventually the girls had been restrained, but during the night they had torn the jackets off, damaging them and ripping their clothes.

The prosecutor at the trial, The Hon. C Mann, QC, requested the highest possible penalty be imposed for all except one girl, Annie Smithwick, who was said to have been coerced into joining in. Mr Beddome was happy to oblige. He sentenced Smithwick to one week in prison and the rest to six months with hard labour. This time there was no giggling in court. The girls wept during the trial, pleading that they would not offend again. On hearing the sentence they were so overcome with emotion that one girl had to be carried out.

After serving her second prison sentence, Harriet still had to complete her time at the Industrial School. She would have been due for release from there early in 1884. The experience of Reformatory and prison with hard labour had, unsurprisingly, failed to have a reforming influence on her. What was she to do? Now that she had a prison record, she was unemployable.

By February that same year she was before Mr Beddome in the Police Court again, charged along with several other girls with "loitering". She was fined £2. She received another £2 fine for the same offence in June, again in November, and then again in April 1885. In August that year Mr Beddome fined her £2 for using indecent language. If she hadn't done so already, she was well on the way to joining the prostitutes who frequented west Adelaide.

But then her name disappears from the Australian newspapers. The report of her court appearance in August 1885 is the last mention of Harriet in Adelaide. Sometime between that date and August 1888 she arrived in Colchester.

What made Harriet decide to seek out her parents of whom, as far as we know, she had no memory, and siblings she had never met? Had she herself concluded that this was a way of escaping the downward spiral that she was now on? As her situation in Adelaide became more and more desperate, did she think that her parents would, or should, support her?

Did her Aunt Mary Ann, or some other relative concerned about her welfare, encourage her to go? Or could it be that the death of her aunt and uncle within weeks of each other in 1887 was what sent her looking for her family in England? Given the trajectory she was on, it seems unlikely that she could have kept out of trouble between 1885 and 1887 if she had remained in Adelaide.

Could the marriage of Clara Lindrum in October 1885, or that of Frederick Lindrum to Harriet's cousin Harriet Atkin in 1886 have prompted her, for some reason, to leave Adelaide? And who paid for her passage to England? Even travelling third class it would have cost her in the vicinity of £20, a considerable sum for someone in Harriet's situation.

It may have been a co-incidence that David Whybrew left the army in August 1885 at his own request. But it's tempting to wonder if his decision to leave and spend more time at home might have had some connection with Harriet's troubles and her impending arrival. Without knowing what date she arrived, we'll probably never know if the two events were linked. Unfortunately many of the United Kingdom's incoming passenger lists from before 1890 were destroyed in 1900 in a sudden bout of efficiency by a zealous employee of the Board of Trade.

Harriet was not the only South Australian to decide to visit her family in England around this time. By a strange co-incidence, Mr Samuel Beddome requested, and was granted, nine months leave of absence from his position as Police Magistrate in November 1885, for "health reasons". Reading between the lines he seems to have been suffering a form of burnout or depression. After travelling around the Australian colonies for several months and feeling no better, he sailed for England in March 1886, returning to Adelaide in good spirits in July after visiting friends and family "in the old country".

When Harriet arrived in England, Susan and David, with their six children, were living in Burlington Road in Colchester. David was working as a labourer with the army, and it's likely that Eliza, now in her late teens, was already employed as a seamstress. Alice and Rose, being close in age, were happy with each other's company. The three young boys, John, Henry and William, ensured there was never a quiet moment in the house.

Susan had begun supplementing the family's income by working at home as a laundress. Until the invention of the electric-powered washing machine in the early 1900s, washing clothes was a long, laborious task. Families saved up their laundry for as long as possible so that it could all be done together, typically once every few weeks if they had enough clothes to last that long. If they could afford to pay someone like Susan to do their laundry, they did.

Many homes in working class areas like Burlington Road had no running water on tap, so the water Susan needed probably had to be carried from a pump or well. It then had to be heated in a copper, a large metal boiler set in a brick firebox in the corner of the kitchen or scullery, until it was hot enough to dissolve the soap and the grease on the clothes. Susan would have needed to be up very early in the morning to light the fire in order to have the water ready for doing the laundry after breakfast.

The clothes (which must often have been quite malodorous) had to be sorted, soaked if necessary, treated for stains, then washed in a wooden tub or stone trough, using a bar of lye soap and a wooden 'dolly' to agitate and pound them. White clothes and sheets, as well as tougher, dirtier work clothes, could be boiled in successive loads in the copper itself. After being put through a wringer, rinsed twice and starched if necessary, the wet clothes were wrung out and flattened using a mangle, and then hung to dry - outside in fine weather, but inside on racks when it rained.

Once the clothes were dry Susan would have ironed them using a heavy flat iron heated on the stove. She may have had several irons, so that one could be in use while the others were re-heating. The whole process of soaking, washing, drying and ironing took several days, so she probably started the laundry process on Monday in order to have the ironing done by Saturday afternoon. It then had to be returned to the customers. It was backbreaking work, particularly for someone who was pregnant so much of the time.

Nevertheless, being a laundress was one of the few occupations open to a married woman like Susan. Taking in laundry would have allowed her to work at home while looking after the children, though she would likely have been occupied with washing and ironing from early in the morning to late at night. The children might have been called on to help with tasks such as carrying water, turning the mangle and hanging clothes. They would have lived with lines of wet washing, the steam from the copper and the smell of damp clothes and laundry soap.

Because laundresses were often poorly educated, physically strong, independent women who effectively ran their own businesses, they were considered 'unladylike' and lacking in social respectability. As a soldier's wife, Susan already came close to the bottom of the social ladder. Being a laundress simply added another layer to her outsider status.

We can only imagine by what process Harriet found her way from her port of arrival to her parent's home

Colchester. We don't know whether David or Susan, a family friend, or perhaps even one of David's extended family from Colchester, met her along the way, escorted her to the house and introduced her to each of her siblings. We don't even know for sure that the family knew she was coming.

What went through each of the Whybrews' minds as they met the teenage Harriet for the first time? For Susan, no matter how hard she had tried over the years to imagine Harriet growing up, there would surely have been the shock of seeing the child she forever recalled as an infant, now standing before her as a young woman. In the storm of emotions that must have taken place in her heart, did joy or apprehension, relief or guilt, or some other emotion win out?

For David, perhaps, there would have been a strong impulse to seek some family likeness in Harriet's appearance to settle his doubts about who her father really was. What did he discover, what conclusion did he reach? As an older man, did he find it easy or difficult to establish a relationship with this young woman?

For Harriet herself there would have been a frantic re-arranging of her mental images of this family she had never seen as she substituted each imagined face with the real thing. And she would have had all the same cultural readjustments to make that Susan had once had in coming from Australia to England.

Of all the children, Eliza might have had the most difficulty in coming to terms with Harriet's sudden inclusion in the family. Although she was younger than Harriet, she had been the eldest child in the family for her whole life, no doubt with an eldest child's sense of responsibility. The gap in age between herself and Alice, created by the deaths in infancy of her brother David and sister Rosina, set her apart from the rest of the children.

She had witnessed more dramas and grief than many girls her age, even if she had not always been old enough to understand what was happening. With David spending so much of his time at the barracks, she could well have become something of a confidante to Susan. With her quiet disposition, she probably understood better than anyone how to manage Susan's temper. But did Susan tell her everything? Was she even aware that she had an older sister living in Australia, before Harriet arrived?

The whole family must have found Harriet's arrival both exciting and disorienting. Adjusting their lives to accommodate a turbulent teenager with a two year history of institutional life was bound to be a challenge even for the best of families. And it seems that Susan and David were not faring well at this stage. Susan had apparently turned to alcohol as an escape from her cares. David no doubt found life in a suburban household chaotic and stressful after the ordered life of the barracks. There were heated arguments between them.

Their conflict came to a head in August 1888. David arrived home one Saturday to a household in chaos, as it had been so often in past weeks. Susan, who was pregnant at the time, pleaded with him for money, ostensibly to pay for some beans that she'd bought that day. He angrily accused her of drinking away the money he'd already given her, of neglecting the house and the children. They began arguing, so loudly and violently that their neighbour, Jane Hubbard, went out of her back door and down the lane-way behind the house to see what was happening. She arrived at the Whybrews' window just in time to see David land a fist in Susan's face, leaving her bloodied, while the children cowered in the background. Another blow hit Susan in the chest.

In court, charged with assault, David did not attempt to deny that he'd struck Susan. There was little point; she still had a black eye and Jane Hubbard was present as a witness to tell her story. Instead he made a statement that could have been copied straight from the one he'd delivered in the Adelaide courts twenty years previously:

"He was very sorry to stand in the position in which he was now placed, but really it was not his fault. He had served twenty years in Her Majesty's Army and was discharged with a good conduct medal, and he had never up to the present had a stain upon his character."

He claimed that Susan had been drunk every day of the previous week, despite having seven children to care for (a slight exaggeration, given Eliza and Harriet's age). After she'd spent all the money he'd given her on drink, he'd refused to give her any more, at which point she took up a tea cup and "threatened to knock his brains out". He had hit her, he admitted, but it was in self defence.

He then called on Harriet and Eliza to act as witnesses to Susan's drunkenness. They seemed quite ready to support his case, reportedly saying that they led 'wretched lives'. (Harriet's willingness to act as witness against her mother suggests that she had been with the family for some time.)

The ironically named Wilson Marriage Esq., Chairman of the Magistrates Bench, said that the members of the Bench were satisfied that David did indeed strike his wife, but he had had 'great provocation'. He ought to know that no amount of provocation could justify him hitting her, but the Bench would refrain from fining him, instead binding him over to the sum of £5 to keep the peace for six months.

Neither Susan nor David were happy with this outcome. Susan asked the Bench for a separation order, but the Chairman said that the present court couldn't deal with that. David then suggested that the Bench bind his wife over to keep the peace as well, but the Magistrates' Clerk explained that couldn't be done either. All that David could do would be to summon her if she struck him again.

It seems likely, given that Susan was not someone to take any sort of abuse complacently, that this was the only time that David had struck her with such violence, though there may well have been previous fights. David had got his own nose bloodied going to Susan's defence when she was involved in her altercation with James Foggarty in Canterbury. But evidently their relationship had become strained to breaking point by living together after years of David being away in the barracks most of the time.

"An Unhappy Family", the Essex Standard headed its report of the case on 18 August. Perhaps it was the same newspaper reporter from the Essex Standard who titled his court report, on 20 October, "A Miserable Family." This time, however, it was Susan's turn to be summonsed for assault, not by David but by Harriet.

The previous Saturday afternoon, Harriet said, she had arrived home and went upstairs to wash herself. Susan had called out after her that Harriet should have paid her for the collar and cuffs that she had washed for her.

Susan's expectation that Harriet should either do her own washing or pay for any extra effort was not unwarranted. Detachable white lacy collars and cuffs, in vogue at the time, needed to be washed separately and with care. The laundry and ironing Susan took in as a way of supplementing the family income gave her a keen sense of the value of her labour in washing the collar and cuffs. With five younger children to care for she was not prepared to treat Harriet as a child.

Harriet came back downstairs and they got into an argument, which quickly escalated. Susan took a plate off the mantelpiece and began chasing Harriet around the table, attempting to hit her and screaming at her to "clear out of the house".

David had been present and had seen what happened, and Harriet called on him as a witness. However as Susan's husband he was not eligible by law to give evidence in court against her. Harriet then called on her sister Eliza, who confirmed that her mother and sister had been fighting, and added that she had done her best to separate them.

Susan, in her defence, said that if Harriet had been hit, it was "in a rush" of emotion on her part. She was treated "most shamefully both by her daughter and her husband" and "didn't know whether she was the missus of the house or her daughter. When she was ill she had to get up and do the washing herself."

After the Bench bound her over to keep the peace for six months she declared that she would rather be separated from her husband than live in the house where he was - truly "a miserable family". But the newspaper's attempt to convey Susan's belligerence towards her daughter and husband in a slightly comical tone missed the deep vein of unhappiness that Susan was evidently experiencing at this time.

Her cry that she "didn't know whether she was missus of the house" was not trivial. For the first eighteen years of her marriage she had, of necessity, been in charge of the household while David came and went from his residence at the barracks. As her role model she had had her mother Catherine, unwillingly thrust into being head of an all-female household by the death of her husband. Now, suddenly, Susan was having to adjust to the presence both of David, who surely considered himself the head of the household, and Harriet, who showed her no respect.

Perhaps Susan also felt envious of her eldest daughter, still young and attractive, with her freedom to come and go as she pleased, freedom to spend Saturday afternoons with her friends, freedom from the responsibility of caring for others. How long it must have seemed since she herself had that freedom.

It's not difficult to imagine that Harriet had come to England with a rather rosy picture of what life in her own family would be like. What she encountered in Burlington Road must have quickly disenchanted her. It's likely that she was immature and self-focused for her twenty years, even if she was street wise. Perhaps Susan's attempts to re-establish herself as mistress of the house provoked in Harriet memories of Matron McColl and her days in Magill. At the same time, the steaming heaps of laundry and dripping clothes around the house must also have brought back unpleasant recollections for her. Perhaps she saw Susan, bent over her washtub and ironing sheets and garments with hands made raw by the work, as a prisoner in her own house. We are all capable of forming such contradictory impressions.

In many ways Harriet had much in common with Susan. Both were strong willed and quick tempered. Both had experienced much of their childhood without a father. They had both spent time in their teenage years on the streets of Adelaide, in conflict with the law, mixing with prostitutes, but answering to no-one. But their similarities made it more likely that any disagreement between the two would flare into a major row.

We can't read too much into newspaper reports, but it does seem evident from what was allegedly said in these two cases that neither Susan nor David found any joy in their marriage or wanted to remain in it. David apparently thought Susan slovenly and negligent of her duties, while Susan must have resented David's unwillingness to accept any responsibility for their problems, falling back as he always did on his dutiful service to his Queen and country. Why then, did they continue to live together and go on producing children?

The most likely answer is that they had no choice. Divorce was both expensive and difficult in the 19th century. Under the Divorce and Matrimonial Causes Act of 1857, a man wishing to divorce his wife would have to prove in court that she had been unfaithful. The person with whom she was alleged to have committed adultery had to appear as a co-respondent so that damages and costs might be claimed against him, the underlying assumption being that the adulterer had interfered with, or stolen, the property of another man - that is, his wife. Even if he had grounds for divorce, a labourer like David could afford neither to hire a lawyer to help him weave his way through the lengthy proceedings nor to take time off work to spend weeks in court.

A woman in an unhappy marriage had even less chance of ending it. To divorce her husband Susan would not only have had to prove adultery on David's part (of which, it should be said, there is no evidence), but would also have had to produce evidence of his cruelty, incest, bigamy or desertion. The level of abuse required to convince a court of cruelty was high, given the prevailing attitude that "all men knock their wives around a bit". An act passed in 1853 limited the amount of force a man might use against his wife and children but certainly didn't ban all forms of domestic violence. The best she could hope for would be a separation order from the courts, which would allow her to live apart and request maintenance payments of up to a quarter of his income. Even this would require evidence of brutality. Desertion as a result of a husband's service in the army was not recognised as reason for a divorce or even a separation order.

By long-standing custom, once a woman married, everything she had came under her husband's control, including not only her property but also her body and her sexuality. In 1884 women in Britain were given the right to manage their own property and income, but the right to control their own bodies remained limited. In marriage a man had a 'conjugal right' to intercourse with his wife. In theory a woman could also claim her 'conjugal rights' to her husband's body, but in practice it was usually the husband's will that prevailed in the marriage bed. Without the availability of effective contraception many women continued to bear children every couple of years no matter how loveless their marriages might be.

Susan and David appear to have remained faithful to each other, despite their misery, and so had no grounds for a divorce, even if they could have afforded one. Hence their futile pleas to the magistrates to grant them a separation order. Perhaps what we are seeing here was a passing storm in their marriage, an eruption of the long-standing strains produced by the life that David's years of armed service had forced them to lead, plus the added strain of Harriet's return. They lacked a cache of good times behind them to remember and fall back on when things were difficult. Nor did either of them have a childhood model for how to sustain a long-lasting marriage, given the early deaths of one or both their parents.

Declining health and strength may also have played a part in their conflict. David was now 50 years old, Susan was 40 and pregnant, thus her reference to "when she was ill" during her evidence in court. The toll on her physical health of nine previous pregnancies could not have been small.

She gave birth to a son, Alfred, not long after her court appearance in October 1888. He lived only a few months. If Susan was drinking heavily, as David suggested, this may have affected both her unborn child's health and her own ability to care for him adequately after he was born.

The outcome for this "miserable family" was that Harriet did indeed move out, after an unknown length of time trying to live with her parents. In 1890, when she appeared in court again over a dispute with another young woman, she was said to be living in Magdalen Street in Colchester. Whether this relieved some of the pressure that Susan and David felt can only be guessed.

Chapter 10

The end of an era – 1890-1914

Whatever health problems Susan faced, she proved strong enough to overcome them. By 1890, at the age of 42, she had outlived four of her seven sisters. Only Catherine, Eliza and possibly Bridget remained, though Bridget disappears from the public record after a hospital admission in Adelaide in 1867. Whether Susan still received news from her sisters in South Australia or Eliza in Scotland is unknown.

She may not have heard that her old nemesis, Samuel "Sammy" Beddome, had finally retired from the Police Courts in Adelaide, after 33 years in his post. His retirement in August 1890 came just months after the tragic death by suicide of his son Henry. But Susan may well have heard the startling and widely reported news in 1895 that women in her home state of South Australia could now vote and even sit in Parliament, something that would not happen in Britain for another couple of decades.

Her life in the 1890s revolved around her family and the goings on in the streets and barracks of Colchester. As was common in the days when women started child-bearing in their early twenties and continued until menopause, Susan was still producing children herself when her first grandchild arrived.

Late in 1890, just months after Susan gave birth to another daughter, Ellen (known to the family as Nellie), Harriet married Henry Malone. Like Harriet, Henry Malone had spent little of his childhood with his parents. Although born in India, he had been brought up by his grandparents in Colchester while his mother travelled with his father, a soldier in the British army. Harriet's marriage to Henry seems to have had a stabilising effect on her. Her name does not appear again in the newspapers.

Harriet and Henry's first child, Cissy, was born in the autumn of 1892. They were still living in Colchester at the time. Had the rift between Susan and Harriet been mended enough for Susan to enjoy her new status as a grandmother? Sadly Cissy lived only a few months.

David, now working as a watchman and labourer for the Royal Engineers Department in Colchester, slipped and fell from a ladder in March 1891. He injured his ankle badly enough to be a patient in the hospital when the census was taken in April. Susan was at home in Burlington Road with the six children still living there (Eliza, Alice, John, Henry, William and Ellen). She continued to work as a laundress.

At the end of 1891 Susan and David's daughter Eliza married a soldier of sorts, though probably not of a kind that David would have recognised or even approved. William Beales, a porter working for a grocery store in Colchester, came from a family that had joined the Salvation Army early in its history, and he was an active member of the Colchester Salvation Army band. Eliza soon became a leading member of the Salvation Army Citadel in Colchester.

It would be fascinating to know what Susan and David made of Eliza's involvement in the Salvation Army. Susan had been brought up in her parent's Catholic faith, and she adopted her husband's Anglican tradition at marriage. David at least would have been expected by the army to attend church regularly. But neither Susan nor David seem to have been active church members. Eliza was taking a step away from the family, socially and spiritually, in joining the Salvation Army, which in those days was still seen as a radical sect. Yet she was also repeating her mother's story of changing her religious affiliation when she married.

The Salvation Army had a presence in Colchester from the early 1880s. They met initially in one of the town's theatres. In 1882 William Booth, the Salvation Army's founder, bought the skating rink in Colchester as a meeting hall, after its owner's business failed. Meetings, particularly those held in the open air, were frequently disrupted by heckling, bottles being thrown and other unruly behaviour. The Salvation Army's use of military terminology for its buildings and officers did not go down well in a garrison town like Colchester. Despite this, William Booth preached in Colchester several times.

The Salvation Army also had a presence in South Australia from 1880, setting up their headquarters on Light Square where the prostitutes and their customers gathered. One of their missions focused on rescuing young girls from prostitution and returning them to their families. It's quite likely that Harriet had encountered them on the streets of Adelaide during her time of 'loitering'. They may have had some influence, or even played an active role, in her returning to her parents, though no evidence has come to light to confirm this.

Susan's appearances in the police courts continued on into the 1890s and 1900s. In June 1892 the Essex Standard reported that "Rose Whybrew (sic), wife of David Whybrew, Burlington Road" had been summonsed for assaulting her neighbour, Harriet Kettle. In her defence her lawyer, H. W. Jones, asked that the case be withdrawn as his client was "in a very delicate state of health" and an amicable settlement had already been reached between the two women. While it may be that Susan's 15 year old daughter Rose was the defendant, it seems more likely that it was Susan herself. She would have been pregnant with her next child, James, at the time, thus the reference to her delicate state of health. James was born at the end of 1892, but lived only a few days.

It is worth pausing here to look at Susan's "legal career" and ask what led to her being so often in court. Over the forty years between 1865 and 1905 she was involved in at least 13 separate court cases. (There may have been others that have not yet come to light.) In seven of these cases she was the prosecutor, in four the defendant, and twice she was a witness to an incident in which she had played an active role.

With a couple of exceptions, each case involved Susan getting into a verbal, and sometimes physical, conflict with a neighbour, family member or acquaintance. She was assaulted, or claimed to have been assaulted, several times, but she was also charged with assault twice.

On seven occasions she would have been visibly pregnant at the time she went to court. That may have been merely by chance, given that she gave birth to 14 children over the same period. But perhaps lack of sleep, frustration with her lot in life or the physical strain of being pregnant made her more vulnerable and less able to control her emotions at these times. On the occasion just mentioned her condition led the court to take a more sympathetic view of her case, but otherwise her pregnant state isn't mentioned by the newspaper reporters.

In fact the cases in which she was involved were reported in the dismissive and slightly satirical way that was standard at the time. Court reporters and newspaper editors were generally well-educated, middle class men, who found the goings-on of the working class either trivial or amusing. Judges, too, tended to dismiss cases with a comment such as "They're both as bad as each other."

Because of this it's difficult to assess whether Susan tended to exaggerate her injuries or misuse the courts to settle her grievances. We get a picture of her as an ignorant, argumentative woman who used bad language and lashed out physically when crossed, then skilfully played the victim role in court. She perfectly fitted everyone's image of the typical soldier's wife and laundress. But how much of this is the result of stereotyping of her class by the newspapers?

While Susan may have appeared in the magistrates' courts more often than the average person of the time, the nature of the cases in which she was involved was not unusual. Reports of domestic violence and conflicts between neighbours were the everyday fare of the newspapers in Adelaide, Canterbury and Colchester. (Strangely there are no reports of Susan appearing in court during her time in Ireland. Was this because she remained out of strife there, or did the army somehow keep her out of trouble?) Overcrowding, lack of education, negative attitudes towards women and immigrants and a poor standard of living among the working class probably contributed to this. Laws that sought to uphold "common decency" such as those against the use of obscene language, tended to target the working class.

Despite all this, from her very first case in her teens Susan seems to have viewed the courts as a place to have her complaints heard and her rights upheld rather than somewhere to be avoided. Perhaps this was due either to an ignorance of, or a disdain for, what was considered appropriate behaviour for a woman. But it is probably also a reflection of how strongly she felt the need to be respected as a human being.

Two more grandchildren arrived early in 1893, with the births of Henry Everett Malone to Harriet, and Alice Beales to Eliza. Rosina Beales followed in February 1895. Susan, now aged 47, gave birth to her next child, Ada, in the autumn of the same year.

Susan must have been in the early stages of pregnancy with Ada when she appeared again in court, this time as the complainant. Early one morning in April, the court heard, Susan had been walking by the Camp Gate on Mersea Road, Colchester, when she passed a young woman leaning up against the wall, talking to a soldier. Perhaps the girl's pose was provocative, or perhaps Susan knew something about her. Whatever the case, she couldn't resist making a remark, the nature of which the newspaper left unrecorded.

What she said must have been quite offensive, as the girl, Rose Belfall, allegedly lashed out at Susan and threw her to the ground. The soldier ran off as soon as he saw trouble, and Rose Belfall left shortly afterwards with another girl who had been standing nearby. Susan seems to have come to no harm except to her pride.

The court case was adjourned, awaiting the return from London of two witnesses, perhaps the soldier and the girl. It seems they never arrived, as nothing more was reported about the case.

By this time Susan and David had moved from Burlington Road to 34 Pownall Crescent. Here, on 15 October 1896, barely twelve months after Ada's birth, Susan gave birth to her fourteenth and final child, a daughter named Lily. Perhaps she was born prematurely. Within a few weeks she died, a sad end to Susan's child bearing years. She and David now had nine surviving children, ranging in age from Harriet at twenty eight to one year old Ada.

Soon after this they moved again, to 9 Pownall Crescent, a typical two-up, two-down terrace house in the south of Colchester. Though the house was small, their family was decreasing in size as the older children gradually moved out of home.

The two middle girls, Alice and Rose, both married soon after the move to Pownall Crescent; Alice to Herbert Miller, a carpenter and former soldier from Colchester, in April 1896, and Rose to a London-born bootmaker named George Anthony in June 1897.

The boys too were growing up. The year that Ada was born John, the Whybrews' eldest son, enlisted in the Essex Regiment's 3rd Battalion, a local militia. A year later, when he turned 18, he transferred to the York and Lancaster Regiment.

At barely 5ft 5in (165cm) John was not tall, but he was lithe and fit. He had inherited the dark hair, blue eyes and fair skin of his Irish ancestors. We can imagine that David felt a certain pride, perhaps even nostalgia, seeing his son dressed in regimental uniform. Susan too, must have admired her boy, but perhaps she also felt a mother's natural apprehension about what his future might hold.

However, John's time in the army proved to be quite brief. In August 1897 he was sentenced to 14 days confinement for breaking out of the barracks. In January 1898 he noticed deafness in his left ear, which the army doctor found to be caused by a perforated eardrum. Neither John nor the examining doctor could account for the injury, but the army considered it reason enough for him to be listed as permanently unfit. He returned to his previous occupation as a labourer and bricklayer. Later that year he married Emily Licence, the daughter of a blacksmith. It was not to be a happy marriage. By January 1905 Emily had applied for a separation order from John on the grounds of his violent behaviour towards her when he was drunk.

A month after John's discharge from the army his younger brother Henry, who had previously been working as a porter with Parkinson's Tea Company in Colchester, joined the militia of the 3rd Essex regiment. He too had the Irish looks of his mother's side of the family, but at 17 he was a mere 5ft 4in and 101lbs (45kg), little more than a child. As soon as he was old enough he transferred to the York and Lancaster regiment of the regular army.

Henry must have been aware when he enlisted that a war was brewing and that he was likely to be sent into battle. Tensions between Britain and the Boers of South Africa and Orange Free State, over control of the gold mining industry and the political rights of the Boers, had been increasing for some time. The Boer War (technically the second Anglo-Boer War) between Britain and its colonies on one hand, and the Boers on the other, began in October 1899.

Initially public enthusiasm for the war was high. On 6 October The Essex Standard published a list of the regiments being mobilised, and on 28 October carried a long and moving account of the Royal Irish Fusiliers' departure from Colchester for South Africa. Three days later Susan and David's son Henry transferred to this regiment.

Henry was not immediately posted to South Africa. Instead he was sent to do his training in Bulford camp in Wiltshire. It seems that Henry inherited not just his looks from his mother, but also something of her quick temper. In April 1900 his time in Bulford camp was extended by 6 months due to his incarceration in military prison for striking a superior officer.

Susan herself was still getting into conflicts even now that she was in her fifties. In November 1900, not long after Henry finished his prison sentence, she charged a neighbour, Annie Jukes, with assaulting her. Annie had accused Susan of "saying bad things about her" to her employers, the couple with whom she lived. Allegedly she then hit Susan in the face and chased her into the Whybrews' kitchen, where she continued to assault her. Annie, in her defence, said that Susan had hit her first. In the absence of witnesses, it was one woman's word against the other, and the case was dismissed.

That same November, not long after the court case, Susan's sister Eliza Murphy died in Scotland. Jeremiah Murphy had died just three months earlier. Eliza and Jeremiah had at least ten children, with the youngest, Lily, still only a toddler when she died. After her death the family seems to have broken up. News of her death, if Susan ever received it, must have caused her great sadness.

In January 1901 Henry again found himself in military detention, this time for failing to appear on parade and for "negligently" losing some of his equipment. Henry was still sitting in the guard room waiting to be tried when the news broke that Queen Victoria had died.

For David, Victoria's death, though not unexpected, was likely a cause for sorrow. Though he professed his steadfast service to the Queen for his own benefit at times, his loyalty was probably heartfelt. For Susan, whatever her thoughts about the British Monarchy, Victoria's death marked the end of an era. Susan's father John had still been serving time as a convict in New South Wales when Victoria ascended to the throne. She had known no other sovereign. As for Henry, he now found himself serving the new King, Edward VII, known as 'Bertie', a man with a reputation for being a playboy rather than for political astuteness.

After serving his prison sentence in Wiltshire, Henry was transferred to barracks in Dublin. In July 1901 he was finally posted to the war in the Transvaal. The 1st Battalion of the Royal Irish Fusiliers in which he served had the task of protecting the crucial railway line in Springfontein, a mixed farming area not unlike much of his mother's home state of South Australia. Springfontein was also the site of one of the notorious concentration camps set up by the British for Boer and Black African internees, mostly women and children.

By this stage the war had lost its popularity in Britain. Reports of horrendous conditions in the concentration camps, coupled with the cost of the war in terms of both men and money, had soured the public attitude. One estimate puts the total cost of the war to Britain at over £200,000,000 and 21,144 military casualties. Nearly

28,000 Boer civilians died in the concentration camps along with unnumbered thousands of Black Africans.

Nearly two thirds of the casualties among the soldiers died from disease rather than battle wounds. Typhoid and dysentery were rife. Early in 1902, just a few months before the war came to an end, Susan and David received the dreadful news that on 9 February their son Henry had succumbed to an infection whilst serving in Springfontein. He was buried close to where he died.

The news must have been devastating to the whole family. David was a soldier, he had seen action in New Zealand and understood the risks, but he'd come through uninjured. Most of his time in the military had been spent in policing roles, where the greatest risk he faced was catching venereal disease from the local women or being arrested for drunken misbehaviour.

Susan, though married to a soldier for 30 years, had never seen the army in action or had to worry that her husband might be injured or killed. Now their son was dead, buried before his twenty first birthday besides some foreign railway track. Who knows what he had gone through before he died.

They might have found it a comfort to know that his grave in the British Army cemetery in Springfontein was later marked, like all the others, with a simple headstone bearing his name and battalion. Perhaps it was just as well that they were never able to visit the cemetery, to read the name inscribed on the headstone: "Pte H. Whyburn, 1st R. Irish Fus." The engraver had evidently been unable to read the name scrawled on his list by some army officer.

Perhaps they felt thankful that Henry's brother John was permanently unfit for military service, and their younger son William, now 18, showed no inclination to become a soldier. Their girls Alice and Rose had not chosen to marry soldiers. They might hope to keep the rest of their family around them. That hope was to be dashed over the next few years.

Alice and her husband Herbert were the first to announce their intention to migrate to the United States, no doubt hoping, like millions of others from Britain and Europe, to find better opportunities there for themselves and their children. Herbert travelled ahead of the family, arriving in New Brunswick, Canada in April 1905 aboard the Virginian. He then crossed into the United States and settled in Chicago. Alice, their 4 year old daughter Alice Frances and 1 year old Bessie Mary made their own way to Canada aboard the Tunisian, arriving in Quebec in August 1905.

Though Bessie arrived safely in Canada with her mother, her name disappears from the records at that point. She is absent from the census taken in the North West Provinces in 1906, which shows Alice and her daughter Alice living in the Winnipeg district of Manitoba. It seems likely she died soon after they arrived. The promise of a successful new life in America was already falling apart for Herbert and Alice.

Possibly Alice had delayed her travels in order to attend her younger brother William's wedding to Adelaide Williams in Colchester in the autumn of 1905. And it may have been a wedding present for William or a farewell present for Alice that became the focus of yet another court case for Susan in July 1905. She and her son John got into an altercation over a framed photograph with a young canvasser from a photographic company, named James McBirnie. In court Susan accused McBirnie of smashing the picture, then throwing her against the washing copper and beating her across the arm with the long heavy copper-stick. McBirnie, for his part, denied hitting Susan and accused John Whybrew of assaulting him. He lost the case and was fined 15 shillings plus costs.

In June 1907 Susan and David's daughter Rose and her husband George Anthony decided to follow Alice and Herbert to the USA. After travelling with their infant son George to Canada they crossed through St Albans, Vermont to Port Huron in Michigan in October and continued on to Chicago, to Alice Miller's home in 48th Avenue.

To Susan, with her limited education, America must have seemed as far away as Australia. It's unlikely that she expected to ever see her two daughters and their children again. At twenty she had probably thought little about what it meant to her mother Catherine when she and her sister Eliza left Adelaide with their soldier husbands, never to return. Now, in middle age, life had turned full circle and with her own two daughters gone, she might have felt a pang of sympathy with her mother.

One consolation was that news travelled more quickly in 1907 than it had in 1870. A letter could be sent from London to Chicago in under two weeks. The first trans-Atlantic telegraph line had been laid in 1866. Although the cost of a telegram was prohibitive in those days, by the early 1900s ordinary people could send and receive important messages by this means.

Was it by letter or by telegram, then, that Susan and David learned of the death of their daughter Alice in Chicago shortly before Christmas 1909? And did Alice's husband Herbert or her sister Rose break the news to them?

By the following March Herbert had remarried, to an Irish girl named Alice McKeon. His haste in remarrying was not as callous as it sounds. He had a 9 year old daughter to care for, and no family other than Rose to help him. He and his new wife moved out of the house in 48th Avenue, leaving Rose and George and their son still living there.

Life in Colchester continued on despite the sadness caused by Henry and Alice's deaths. Susan and David's second youngest daughter Ellen married George Howard, a soldier and musician, in the autumn of 1910. The newly married couple moved to Aldershot, where it seems George lived in the barracks while Ellen stayed in her own house among a community of other army wives.

David was now over seventy and Susan sixty. Of the fourteen children born to them, only seven (Harriet, Eliza, Rose, John, William, Ellen and Ada) were still alive when the national census was taken in April 1911. Ada, now 16, still lived at home. David described himself on the census as "General labourer" with "pensioner" added as an afterthought. As a former soldier he received an army pension.

Rather surprisingly, the word "nurse" appears as Susan's occupation. Although she had no formal nursing qualifications, she may have found employment nursing an invalid or elderly person in their own home, or acting as a nursing assistant in an institution. But it's possible that David's health was failing and she had become his nurse at home.

In 1913 news of another tragedy might have reached Colchester. David and Susan's six year old grandson George, son of Rose and George Anthony, died in Chicago at the end of April. He was buried in the same cemetery as his aunt, Alice Miller, at Forrest Home.

What became of Rose and George after this is a mystery. George received call-up papers from the US army in 1917, sent to the address in 48th Avenue in Chicago. Rose's name appears as his next of kin, but at another address in Congress Street. The papers were never signed. Although George appears to be living with Rose in the 1910 census, someone named George Anthony with very similar biographical details to George appears as an inmate of a Chicago psychiatric hospital in 1910, and remained a psychiatric hospital patient until his death in 1941. It's possible he was recorded on the census twice, for instance if Rose expected him to soon return from hospital. After 1917 Rose's name becomes untraceable in the records. Did she remarry, or return to England? Or did she too die in Chicago?

In the spring of 1913 Susan and David's youngest daughter Ada married Joseph Metson. For the first time in their forty five years of married life Susan and David were alone at home together. The strains caused by frequent moves at the whim of the army, lives lived separately in and out of barracks and sharing cramped and overcrowded houses were gone. They had been in Pownall Crescent long enough to know their neighbours and perhaps become part of a community. They might, then, have looked forward to a few years of peace and enjoyment of the calmer relationship that often comes to couples with old age. But David's ill health was not the only dark cloud. Another war was on the horizon.

Chapter 11

Exhaustion – 1914-1921

The residents of Colchester must have been particularly aware of the preparations for war. So many of them, including Susan and David's family, belonged to army families or were associated in some way with the army presence in the town. As early as 1909 the British War Office asked the Red Cross and the Order of St John to establish Voluntary Aid Detachments, trained in nursing and first aid, in case they should be needed. Long before war was declared the numbers of soldiers in the town began to swell. Susan's daughter Eliza and her husband William Beales had a soldier and his wife lodging with them when the census was taken in 1911. Everyone knew that a war was coming.

When the war did finally begin in August 1914, many expected it to be over within months. No-one was prepared for the four years of ongoing slaughter that would leave millions dead on the battlefields and many more dead among the civilians of towns and villages across Europe.

Many young men joined up in those early days, eager to fight for their king and country against 'the Huns'. Over half a million enlisted within the first two months, including Susan's grandsons, William Beales and Henry Everett Malone. As soldiers flooded into Colchester, the barracks were overflowing and local people were asked to billet soldiers in their own homes, even if it meant having men sleeping on the floor. The population of Colchester doubled.

Even Susan and David's oldest son John seems to have joined up again in October 1914, despite having previously been declared unfit for service because of his perforated eardrum. His estranged wife Emily had died the previous year, and according to family his sister Eliza and her husband William Beales took on the care of his daughter Emily. He enlisted in the Army Veterinary Corps which was charged with looking after the millions of horses, dogs, pigeons and other animals that the army used in its war effort.

As a member of the Vet corps he would have had various roles, from feeding and transporting the animals, to slaughtering the injured and burying the dead when required. This was no small task. In 1916 at Verdun 7000 horses were killed in one day alone, and over the course of the war nearly half a million horses and mules perished.

John's time in the army was once again brief. He was discharged from the army three months later, in February 1915, perhaps due to the same deafness that ended his earlier army career.

John's brother William, who was almost thirty years old when the war began, also enlisted early in its course. William and his wife Adelaide were living in Cambridge at the time, 64 kilometres from Colchester. William worked as a carman for a mineral water company in Cambridge, driving a horse-drawn delivery van. Adelaide seems to have had the care of an elderly lodger in their home. They may have lived in Cambridge due to William's work or perhaps for more personal reasons.

Adelaide was at least fifteen years older than William. It was unusual for a man to marry a woman so much older than himself (though Adelaide was no older than his sister Harriet) and they may have wanted to avoid being the subject of gossip.

Their marriage was childless, although Adelaide may have had a son or stepson from a previous relationship. A young soldier, Henry Lawrence, named a "Mrs Whybrew" as his mother and next of kin on his enlistment papers, and his discharge address at the end of the war was the same as Adelaide Whybrew's address on William's papers.

Like his brother John, William originally joined the Army Veterinary Corps, where his experience with horses would have been put to good use. He was sent to the front in France in December 1914. He transferred to the 13th Battalion of the Alexandra, Princess of Wales Own (Yorkshire) regiment, and then to the 9th (service) battalion, which was part of the 69th brigade of the 23rd division of Lord Kitchener's so called "new army".

He experienced the nightmare of the trenches of France for three years. In November 1917 his battalion moved to Italy to support the Italian resistance, returning to France in September 1918 to join the 74th Brigade of the 25th division.

Susan and David once again found themselves anxiously waiting for news of a son from the battlefield. If they or Adelaide received letters from him, they haven't survived. But the war was no longer just a distant event. The introduction of aircraft meant that for the first time in history, factories, army depots and civilians at home became a target. The use of zeppelins allowed the Germans to carry out air raids across southern England, their arrival going undetected until the bombs fell.

On the night of Sunday 21 February, 1915, a German bomber pilot dropped a high explosive bomb over Colchester. It landed in the back garden of 41 Butt Road, damaging the back of the house and destroying an empty baby's pram, but fortunately injuring no-one. This first air raid on Colchester happened less than a mile from the Whybrews' house, just across Abbey Fields where the army did its training. The war had suddenly come frighteningly close.

The war also affected supplies of food. As in many cities across Europe, people in Colchester often had to queue for hours to buy staples such as bread, sugar and potatoes. The local newspapers, once padded with reports of gardening shows, school concerts and petty crime, were now full of news of the war and local activities to support the war effort. Each week they printed heroically cheerful letters from men on the battle front to their families at home, and sombre lists of those who would never write home again.

Susan and David's daughter Ellen was the first in the family to receive one of the type-written fill-in-the-blanks letter that they had all been dreading: Army Form B104-82. "It is my painful duty to inform you..." it began. Her husband, George Howard, had been killed in action while serving with the 11th battalion of the Royal Sussex regiment in France. His death on 4 August 1917, somewhere among the devastation of what had once been the woods and market gardens of Ypres and Passchendaele, left her as a widow with a young son to care for.

To an old soldier like David, the war must have seemed incomprehensible in its sheer brutality and the use of technical innovation on an industrial scale. His own training in the use of muskets and hand to hand combat would have been useless in the trench warfare being reported daily in the news. The willingness of military and political leaders to sacrifice thousands of young men's lives to advance just a few metres of ground must also have left him appalled.

David didn't live to see the end of it. He had been ill for some time with a malignant growth in his neck. On 15 October 1917, as winter approached, he died at home in Pownall Crescent. He was 79 years old, a good age for an old soldier. Susan registered his death herself. She signed the death register with an "X" in lieu of her name, an ironic, illiterate kiss marking the end of their long relationship.

David was buried in Colchester cemetery. It would not have been an elaborate funeral - he had no claim to fame, the family were not well off, and there was a war on. He slipped out of the sight of history with the same lack of fanfare that he'd entered it, not far from where he had been born, having outlived all his siblings. A month later Susan's last remaining sister, Catherine Davis, died in Adelaide.

Susan was now on her own. She may well have had no income, if, as is likely, David's pension came to an end at his death. She and David had been married for forty eight years. Though their relationship had been ambiguous, fractious, even stormy at times, they had remained together, and together they had grieved over children lost in infancy, daughters lost to emigration, and a son lost to war. They had children buried on three continents, and in four countries. That tally of countries would soon become five.

A year after David's death, just days before the signing of the armistice which brought the war to an end, Susan received news that William Whybrew, her youngest son Bill, was dead. His wife Adelaide would have been the first to receive the news in the recognisable buff envelope, with it's carefully worded condolences from Their Gracious Majesties, the King and Queen.

Perhaps Adelaide, now living in her home town of Ipswich, wrote to Susan or one of her daughters, or perhaps she visited, bringing the dreadful letter with her. Let's hope that Susan didn't hear of her son's death through the newspapers or from lists of casualties posted on office windows, as some families did.

William Whybrew was killed in action in France on 24 October 1918. Of the 65,000 men who fought in the Yorkshire Regiment, over 7,500 lost their lives during the course of the war. It's likely that William was involved in the decisive "Hundred Days" battle which broke the Germans resolve and ultimately led to the Kaiser's abdication and the signing of the armistice on 11 November. That was probably little consolation to his family.

His wife Adelaide applied for his medals to be sent to her in Ipswich, along with any money owing to him and what few belongings of his were left with the army. William had no grave, no identifiable remains to be buried. His name was later inscribed on the memorial at Vis-en-Artois, in the Pas de Calais north of Paris. His was among 9,847 names of men with no known burial place who fell between August 1918 and the end of the war. His name also appears on the war memorial in Ipswich, but not on the one in Colchester where he grew up and enlisted.

The loss of two sons, Henry in the Boer war and William in the 'Great War', could be seen as the price Susan paid for belonging to British society. In her grief she joined millions of other mothers who had experienced similar losses. But did this shared loss give her, the convict's daughter from the colonies, a greater sense of belonging? Did she earn respect among her neighbours and community for her sacrifice? Or did she remain, to the end, just a common soldier's wife, despised and overlooked?

As the war came to an end, 70 year old Susan was still coming to terms with being a widow. Perhaps she could take some comfort in the fact that her two oldest grandsons had survived the slaughter. William Beales, who enlisted as a member of the machine gun corps, returned home in 1919 after spending time in Afghanistan in the so-called Third Anglo-Afghan. Henry Malone fought and survived the war with the 15th Suffolk regiment. Most of Susan's other eight grandchildren were still living in or around Colchester. None of them would carry on the Whybrew name.

Her widowed daughter Ellen Howard remarried in September 1919, to Alfred Lloyd, a labourer of Islington and she and her son George (Alexander George Ernest Howard) moved to London. Ellen's sister Ada and her husband Joseph Metson were witnesses at the wedding. William Whybrew's widow Adelaide also remarried at the end of 1919, to John Sanders from Ipswich.

As Susan's own health started to deteriorate, she moved from Pownall Crescent to live with her daughter Eliza and her family in Campion Road in Colchester. No doubt she was sometimes an irascible guest but she would have been well cared for.

Whether Susan ever came to share Eliza and Bill's faith is unknowable, but perhaps they had an influence on her, directly or indirectly. Was it simply old age and weariness that saw an end to Susan's appearances in court after 1905? Or could it be that her apparently quieter life as she grew older was a reflection of some change of heart, some new source of fulfilment?

Susan would have been still alive in January 1921 when her granddaughter Rosina married, though she may not have been well enough to attend the wedding in the parish church of St Botolph, Colchester. Rosina, like her grandmother Susan, would leave not only her childhood home, but her childhood religious tradition when she married Thomas Henry Ward, a returned soldier several years older than herself. They moved to his home village of Milnrow in Lancashire and she joined the Church of England.

Susan, at the age of 73, had outlived all her sisters, her husband and half of her children. She had stood up to so many threats to her well-being and sense of dignity, but death was not an annoying neighbour who could be taken to court. Susan died at Bill and Eliza's home on 19 November 1921. Eliza signed the death certificate in a careful, neat hand. Dr Bassano listed "1. Pneumonia 2. Exhaustion" as the causes of death.

Susan's body was laid to rest in the plot besides David's in Colchester cemetery. In death, at least, they found peace together.

Afterword

At times, as I've been writing Susan's story, I've wondered if she would have wanted it told. Have I been fair to her in cobbling together a life from the fragments of information found in government records and newspaper articles? Should I have left some things unsaid? Would she even recognise the person I've described?

The process of reconstructing a life from scattered pieces has its hazards. But Susan wasn't a secretive person, even if she left no personal records or diaries. She didn't hide demurely behind her husband or keep silent when she had something to say. Nothing I've said about her can't be found readily in the public record. I hope that by telling her story I have given her, and other women like her, a recognition that they were denied in their lifetime.

It's likely, perhaps inevitable, that new information about the Mason and Whybrew families will come to light as soon as this book is published. I'll continue to post new material as I find it, on my family history blog, Clogs and Clippers. If you have information you would like to contribute, I'd love to hear from you. You can contact me via the contact form on Clogs and Clippers or by sending an email to stella.budrikis@gmail.com.

If you've enjoyed this book, please tell your friends, and consider leaving a review on the site where you bought it.

Acknowledgements

Many people have been involved in producing this book. The research itself was by no means a solo effort. I'd like to thank Pauline Jepson, John Marsh, Keith Stanley and Nigel Cooper for sharing their own research with me, and for encouraging me along the way through their emailed conversations.

Thank you to the wonderful volunteers at the Unley Library in Adelaide who have transcribed South Australian birth, marriage and death records for me.

Numerous forum members at BritishGenealogy.com have given me tips on doing genealogy research, confirmed or dispelled my hunches, and stimulated me to think along new lines when I've come to a brick wall.

I'm also grateful to all the generous people, too many to name (and mostly anonymous) who have transcribed genealogical information and freely provided historical documents and information on the Internet. It would have been impossible to do the research I've done from here in Western Australia if I hadn't had such a treasure trove of information on-line.

I owe a great debt to those who have helped in the writing and production of this book. Firstly, my husband Gary, who got me started by saying "If there's a book you need to write, then you've got to write it" and who then gave me space to do just that. He has let me bounce ideas off him, discussed background historical information, listened to me talk endlessly about Susan Mason and her family, commiserated with me on the ups and downs of writing a book, read and commented on the first draft and encouraged me to keep going when I felt like giving up.

My dear friend Sue was another who read the first draft. She offered several helpful suggestions on how I might make the story more accessible and enjoyable to readers outside the family.

My daughter Amy not only read and commented on the rough first draft, but used her editorial skills on what I thought was close to the final draft. With her unflinching red pen she provided invaluable suggestions, questions and corrections, and the book is a much more polished text as a result. Others have read the review copy and spotted typos that I'd missed.

My sister Katie Stewart, who has her own book cover business at Magic Owl Design, came up with a fantastic cover. She then provided four equally beautiful alternatives when I was the customer from hell who said "Maybe it needs…". In the end, her original design was just what was needed after all.

When I set out to write this book, I told myself that it would be a learning process, an experiment in writing a long piece after only ever having written short articles. I have certainly been on a steep learning curve. I'm grateful to all those who have generously shared, on-line or in print, their expertise in writing, editing and self-publishing.

Despite all the help I've received, I'm sure there are still errors to be found in the text. If you do find factual errors, typos or formatting problems, please let me know. You can contact me through my family history blog, Clogs and Clippers, or send an email to stella.budrikis@gmail.com.

Stella Budrikis

Appendix 1 Mason Family

John Mason (c1815-22 Jan 1857)
Married Feb 2 1841
Catherine Murphy (c1822-27 Mar 1874)

Their children:

1. **Roseanne Mason**
Born: 1 Dec 1841 Sydney NSW
Died: 1843 Sydney

2. **Mary Ann Mason**
Born: 19 Oct 1842 Sydney
Died: 16 Mar 1887 Adelaide SA
Married: Henry Atkin, 25 Jul 1865

3. **Catherine Mason**
Born: 25 Mar 1844 Sydney
Died: 6 Nov 1917 South Australia
Married: George Davis, 5 Jun 1865

4. **Margaret Mason**
Born: 20 Jul 1845 Adelaide
Died: 20 April 1879 Adelaide
Married: Thomas Atkin, 26 Feb 1866

5. **Rosanne Mason**
Born: 11 Feb 1847 Adelaide
Died: 23 May 1878 Lambton NSW
Married: William Morris, 11 Mar 1868

6. **Susan Mason**
Born: 6 May 1848 Adelaide
Died: 19 Nov 1921 Colchester, UK
Married: David Whybrew, 28 May 1869

7. **Eliza Mason**
Born: 1 Aug 1850 Adelaide
Died: 23 Nov 1900 Edinburgh, Scotland
Married: Jeremiah Murphy, 19 Mar 1869

8. **Jane Mason**
Born: 6 Jul 1852 Adelaide
Died: maybe Feb 1886 South Australia

9 **Bridget Mason**
Born: 6 May 1854 Adelaide
Died: unknown.

Appendix 2 Whybrew family

David Whybrew (Jan 1839-15 Oct 1917)
Married in 1869
Susan Mason (6 May 1848-19 Nov 1921

Their children:

1. **Harriet Whybrew**
Born: 17 Sep 1868 Adelaide SA
Died: 1935 Colchester, Essex, UK
Married: Henry Malone in 1890

2. **Eliza Whybrew**
Born: 10 Dec 1869 Adelaide
Died: 1949 Colchester
Married: William Beales in 1891

3. **David Whybrew**
Born: 1872 Farnham Surrey UK
Died: 18 July 1874 Colchester

4. **Rosina Whybrew**
Born: 1874 Colchester
Died: 18 Oct 1874 Dublin, Ireland

5. **Alice Whybrew**
Born: 10 Sep 1875 Cork, Ireland
Died: 7 Dec 1909 Cook County, Illinois USA
Married: Herbert A Miller, 1896

6. **Rose Whybrew**
Born: 1877 Canterbury, Kent, UK
Died: Unknown (maybe USA)
Married: George Henry Anthony, 1897

7. **Benjamin John (Jack) Whybrew**
Born: 1879 Canterbury
Died: 1941 Colchester
Married: Emily Licence, 1898

8. **David Henry Whybrew**
Born: 1882 Canterbury Kent
Died: 9 Feb 1902 Springfontein South Africa

9. **William Whybrew**
Born: 29 Oct 1884 Sittingbourne Kent Uk
Died: 24 Oct 1918 France
Married: Adelaide Williams, 1905

10. **Alfred Ernest Whybrew**
Born: 1888 Colchester
Died: 1889 Colchester

11. **Ellen (Nellie) Whybrew**
Born: 1890 Colchester
Died: Unknown
Married: (i)George Howard, 1910

(ii) Alfred Lloyd 1919

12. James Whybrew
Born: 1892 Colchester
Died: 1892 Colchester

13. Ada Whybrew
Born: 1895 Colchester
Died: Maybe 1980 Torbay Devon
Married: Joseph Metson, 1913

14. Lily Whybrew
Born: 15 Oct 1896 Colchester
Died: 1897 Colchester

Maps of Adelaide

Extract from 1880 map of Adelaide showing the west end of Adelaide, the Barracks and the City Baths.

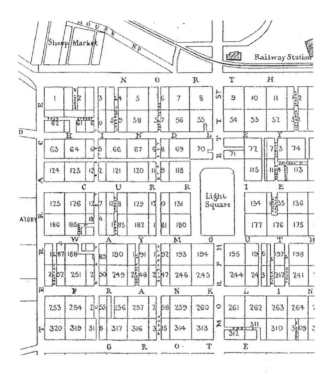

Extract from same map on a slightly larger scale showing the area around Light Square. The Ship Inn was on Acre 120. The complete map is available to view at the Adelaide City Council website.

Endnotes

Abbreviations:

Ancestry.com: Ancestry.com.au, [database on-line]. Provo, UT, USA: Ancestry.com Operations Inc.

BLNA: British Library Newspaper Archive

FS: FamilySearch.org

GRO: General Register Office of England and Wales.

SRA NSW: State Records Authority of New South Wales, Kingswood, New South Wales.

SA: South Australia

SAG library: Genealogy SA Library, Unley, Adelaide, South Australia

TNA: The National Archives, Australia

TNA UK: The National Archives, United Kingdom, Kew, Surrey, England.

Trove: National Library of Australia, *Trove,* Digitised newspapers. For brevity, date of access not included.

Newspapers quoted:

Adelaide Observer (Adelaide, SA : 1843 - 1904)

Adelaide Times (SA : 1848 - 1858)

Chelmsford Chronicle (Chelmsford, Essex, 1901-1950)

Essex Standard (later The Essex Standard, West Suffolk Gazette, and Eastern Counties' Advertiser. Colchester, Essex: 1831 1900)

Essex County Chronicle (previously Chelmsford Chronicle; Chelmsford, Essex: 1884-1919)

Essex Newsman (Chelmsford, England)

Evening Journal (Adelaide, SA: 1869 - 1912)

Quiz (Adelaide, SA : 1889 - 1890)

Roscommon Journal and Western Impartial Observer (Roscommon, Ireland, 1828-1832)

South Australian (Adelaide, SA : 1844 - 1851)

South Australian Advertiser (Adelaide, SA: 1858 - 1889)

South Australian Register (Adelaide, SA: 1839 - 1900)

The Australian (Sydney, NSW : 1824 - 1848)

The Colonist (Sydney, NSW : 1835 - 1840)

The Express and Telegraph (Adelaide, SA: 1867 - 1922)

The Register (Adelaide, SA: 1901 - 1929)

The Sydney Herald (NSW : 1831 - 1842)

The Sydney Monitor (NSW : 1828 - 1838)

The Sydney Morning Herald (NSW : 1842 - 1954)

Whitstable Times and Hearn Bay Herald (Whitstable, Kent: 1864 - 1923)

Note:

I have not included sources for all records of births, deaths and marriages. Most of these are freely available on-line (at least in index form) through sites such as ancestry.com, findmypast.com, FreeBMD.org.uk and genealogy.sa.org.au. Instead I have listed those where the name is indexed in such a way that it is more difficult to find (e.g. Rose Whybrew is listed as "Rose Whybruew" and "Rose Whybren") or where I have added information obtained from the original registration which is not available on-line.

Not a little whore

Mr Beddome's memory: "LETTERS TO PUBLIC MEN. - SAMUEL BEDDOME, POLICE MAGISTRATE." *Quiz.* 31 Jan 1890. Trove. http://nla.gov.au/nla.news-article166370024.

Susan Mason vs Pasquale Nicro: "POLICE COURTS. - ADELAIDE: WEDNESDAY, AUGUST 23. [Before Messrs. 8. Beddome, P.M., H Mildred, S.M., and G. Mavo. J.P.]". *South Australian Register.* 24 Aug 1865. *Trove.* http://nla.gov.au/nla.news-article41020344.

Street musicians - letters to the editor: "STREET MUSICIANS. - TO THE EDITOR." *South Australian Register.* 21 Oct 1867. Trove. http://nla.gov.au/nla.news-article39179902.

Adelaide's west end and Currie St: Patricia Sumerling. "The West End of Adelaide 1870-1936." Professional Historians Association, n.d. http://www.sahistorians.org.au/175/bm.doc/sumerling-west-end-4.doc.

"CURRIE STREET IN THE SIXTIES". *The Register.* 14 Feb 1918. Trove. http://nla.gov.au/nla.news-article60335793.

From Ireland to Adelaide

Catherine Murphy on board the Mary Ann: Ancestry.com. *New South Wales, Australia, Assisted Immigrant Passenger Lists, 1828-1896* Original source: SRA NSW; Kingswood New South Wales, Australia; Entitlement certificates of persons on bounty ships; Series: 5314; Reel: 1315.

John Marshall's ships: "MR. JOHN MARSHALL". *The Sydney Herald*. 24 Dec 1841. Trove. http://nla.gov.au/nla.news-article12872981.

John Mason's arrival: Ancestry.com. *New South Wales, Australia, Convict Indents, 1788-1842*. Original source: State Archives NSW; Series:*NRS 12189*; Item:*[X636]*; Microfiche:*708*.

John's transfer from prison hulk to Parmelia: "WINDING UP OF THE SESSION." *Roscommon Journal, and Western Impartial Reporter*, August 30, 1833. Page 4.

The Great Shame: Keneally, Thomas. *The Great Shame: A Story of the Irish in the Old World and the New.* Random House Australia, 1999.

Ship's surgeon's notes: State Archives NSW; Series:*NRS 12189*; Item:*[X636]*; Microfiche:*708*. *Annotated printed indents,* indexed by Ancestry.com as *New South Wales, Australia, Convict Indents, 1788-1842*[database on-line].

Alexander Fotheringham:1."SRA NSW; Copies of Deeds to Grant to Land Alienated by Grant, Lease or Purchase; Series: NRS 13836; Item: 7/507; Reel: 2705." : Web.

2. Australia. Parliament. Joint Library Committee, and Frederick Watson. *Historical Records of Australia.* Sydney : The Library Committee of the Commonwealth Parliament, 1923. http://archive.org/details/historicalrecord00v17aust.

Wright's store building at Millers Point: Sydney Ports Corporation Heritage Inventory, Study number 4560018, Moore's Wharf Building, http://www.sydneyports.com.au/__data/assets/pdf_file/0014/10292/ Moores_Wharf_Building.pdf

Working with William Doody at Wright and Long: Ancestry.com, *"New South Wales and Tasmania, Australia Convict Musters, 1806-1849"*. Original data:Home Office: Settlers and Convicts, New South Wales and Tasmania; (TNA Microfilm Publication HO10, Pieces 5, 19-20, 32-51); TNA UK. Item: "John Wason" (sic); Class: HO 10; Piece: 35.

William Doody: Ancestry.com, *New South Wales, Australia, Settler and Convict Lists, 1787-1834*. Original source: Home Office: Settlers and Convicts, New South Wales and Tasmania; (TNA Microfilm Publication HO10, Pieces 1-4, 6-18, 28-30); TNA. Item: "William Doody". Class: HO 10; Piece: 29.

Wright and Long assignees charged with insolence: "Police. - MONDAY, AUGUST 29TH., before Mr. GISBORNE". *The Sydney Monitor*. 31 Aug 1836. Trove. http://nla.gov.au/nla.news-article32152099.

British House of Commons report 1838: Commons, Great Britain Parliament House of. Parliamentary Papers, House of Commons and Command. H.M. Stationery Office, 1838. Viewed on-line at Google Books

John Mason certificate of freedom: Ancestry.com. *New South Wales, Australia, Certificates of Freedom, 1810-1814, 1827-1867*. Original data: New South Wales Government. Butts of Certificates of Freedom. NRS 1165, 1166, 1167, 12208, 12210, reels 601, 602, 604, 982-1027. SRA NSW.

John and Catherine's marriage: NSW Registry of Births, Deaths and Marriages, V1841858 91/1841. Transcript provided by P. Jepson.

Rosanna's birth in 1841: NSW Registry of Births, Deaths and Marriages, VOL 133 NO 1796. Transcript.

Childhood illnesses in early Sydney: Lewis, Milton James. *The People's Health: Public Health in Australia, 1788-1950*. Greenwood Publishing Group, 2003.

Mary Ann's birth in 1842: NSW Registry of Births, Deaths and Marriages, VOL 133 NO 2524. Transcript.

Rosanna's death in 1843: NSW Registry of Births, Deaths and Marriages, Index Entry 87/1843V184387 140. Web.

Catherine's birth in 1844: NSW Baptisms (Early Church Records) VOL 134 NO 928 Register -St Mary's Cathedral Roman Catholic Baptisms 1844. Transcript.

The Lady McNaughton typhus outbreak: "Domestic Intelligence. - TYPHUS FEVER. - *The Colonist.* 2 Mar 1837." Trove. http://nla.gov.au/nla.news-article31719145.

Murnane family arrival: SRA NSW. Index to Miscellaneous immigrants. Accessed October 3, 2016. https://www.records.nsw.gov.au/archives/collections-and-research/g uides-and-indexes/miscellaneous-immigrants-index

Bishop Francis Murphy: Hyde, Ken. "Re: Dowdys in Australia". - Genealogy.com. 29 June 2010. Web. Accessed 22 Aug. 2016.

Sydney 1840's recession: "Advertising" The Sydney Morning Herald. 15 Oct 1844. Trove.
http://nla.gov.au/nla.news-article12426289.

Departure from Sydney on the Dorset: "SHIPPING INTELLIGENCE. - ARRIVED. NONE. SAILED". *The Australian.* 23 Dec 1844. Trove. http://nla.gov.au/nla.news-article37120392.

Arrival in Adelaide of the Dorset: "ADELAIDE: THURSDAY, JANUARY 9, 1845. - THE "DORSET" FROM SYDNEY." *South Australian Register.* Trove.
http://nla.gov.au/nla.news-article73843035.

Adelaide building materials etc: Wilkinson, George Blakiston. *South Australia: Its Advantages and Its Resources. Being a Description of That Colony, and a Manual of Information for Emigrants.* J. Murray,1848, 50. Accessed May 28, 2016 at Google Books.

Adelaide sanitation: "Geoff Manning- Insight into South Australian History." Essay 11 - *The First Fleet to South Australia and Aspects of Early Colonial History.* Accessed August 22, 2016. http://www.geoffmanning.net.au/html/single-essays/essay11-first-fle et.html.

Heatwave and white squall: "LOCAL INTELLIGENCE". *Adelaide Observer.* 18 Jan 1845. Trove. http://nla.gov.au/nla.news-article158919659.

Parkhurst Apprentice conflict: 1. "PARKHURST BOYS. - South Australian (Adelaide, SA : 1844 - 1851) - 7 Jan 1845." *Trove.* Accessed June 3, 2016. http://nla.gov.au/nla.news-article71600272.

2. "ADELAIDE: WEDNESDAY, JANUARY 8, 1845. - THE PARKHURST BOYS". *South Australian Register.* 8 Jan 1845. Trove. http://nla.gov.au/nla.news-article73844072.

3. "MEMORIAL BY THE COLONISTS OF SOUTH AUSTRALIA AGAINST THE INTRODUCTION OF CONVICTS". South Australian. 14 Feb 1845. Trove. http://nla.gov.au/nla.news-article71600655.

Convicts in South Australia: Paul Sendziuk, "No Convicts Here: Reconsidering South Australia's Foundation Myth," in *Turning Points: Chapters in South Australian History,* ed. Foster, Robert, and Paul Sendziuk, Wakefield Press, 2012, 42-56.

Irish in South Australia: Richards, Eric. "Irish Life and Progress in Colonial South Australia." *Irish Historical Studies* 27, no. 107 (1991): 216–36.

Colonel Torrens promotion of Irish emigration: "English Extracts. - IRISH IMMIGRATION TO SOUTH AUSTRALIA". *The Colonist.* 1 Jan 1840. Trove. http://nla.gov.au/nla.news-article31724317.

David McLaren's opposition to Catholic Church: "McLaren, David (1785–1850)." In *Australian Dictionary of Biography*. Canberra: National Centre of Biography, Australian National University. Accessed June 3, 2016. http://adb.anu.edu.au/biography/mclaren-david-2412.

Sweepings of the Irish poorhouses: "ADELAIDE: TUESDAY. JULY 3,1855. - THE FEMALE IMMIGRANTS". *South Australian Register.* 3 Jul 1855. Trove. http://nla.gov.au/nla.news-article49298227.

Hindley Street riot of 1855: 1. Adelaide, Hindley Street 5000, and S. A. Australia. "Hindley Street Riot | Adelaidia." Accessed October 6, 2016. http://adelaidia.sa.gov.au/events/hindley-street-riot.

2. "POLICE COURTS. - ADELAIDE: MONDAY, SEPTEMBER 21". *South Australian Register.* 25 Sep 1855. Trove. http://nla.gov.au/nla.news-article49298137.

John's employment: John's occupation at his death was listed simply as "Labourer". However, when his daughter Eliza's death was registered in Scotland in 1900, her father's occupation was recorded as "Mason's labourer". Information supplied by Nigel Cooper, extracted from Deaths in St George, the City of Edinburgh, , p 427, item 1279.

John and Catherine Mason's housing: Adelaide City Council, City Archives, on-line images from Adelaide Assessment Books, 1846-1870, accessed January 5, 2016. http://photosau.com.au/adelaiderates/scripts/home.asp

Peacock's buildings, Grenfell Street: "ST. PATRICK'S SOCIETY." Adelaide Times. 7 May 1849. Trove. http://nla.gov.au/nla.news-article206980639.

Price of land in today's terms: "Measuring Worth - Purchasing Power of the Pound." Accessed October 7, 2016. https://www.measuringworth.com/ukcompare/.

Water in Adelaide's early days: "Water in South Australia's Early Days." Accessed August 22, 2016. http://www.familyhistorysa.info/sahistory/water.html.

Childhood on Currie St

Susan's birth and baptism: "St Patrick's (Adelaide), Catholic Baptisms South Australia, Adelaide district, 1841-1881"; viewed on microfiche, Index 2 (1853-1861), entry 803, "Susanne Mason", SAG library, 25 November 2015.

Fire in Currie Street: "CORONER'S INQUEST." *South Australian Register.* 2 Aug 1852. Trove. http://nla.gov.au/nla.news-article38460596.

"No Title". *South Australian Register.* 4 Aug 1852." Trove. http://nla.gov.au/nla.news-article38458373.

Jane's birth: "St Patrick's (Adelaide), Catholic Baptisms South Australia, Adelaide district, 1841-1881"; viewed on microfiche, Index 2 (1853-1861), entry 1489, "Jane Mason", SAG library, 25 November 2015.

Development of Australian accent: Macquarie University, Sydney, Department of Linguistics. "History and Accent Change," February 19, 2009. http://clas.mq.edu.au/australian-voices/history-accent-change.

William Doody's farm: "Re: Dowdys in Australia - Genealogy.com." Accessed August 22, 2016. http://www.genealogy.com/forum/surnames/topics/dowdy/1333/.

Ancient Order of Foresters: *Ancient Order of Foresters Friendly Society, Adelaide District, 1870-1872: Court Perseverance No. 2221, Established May, 1847, Held at the Norfolk Arms, Rundle Street.* Bro. Shawyer, 1870. Viewed at State Library of Victoria website, http://handle.slv.vic.gov.au/10381/187601

John Mason sings at Court Perseverence: "REPRESENTATION OF WILLUNGA". *Adelaide Observer.* 3 Nov 1855. Trove. http://nla.gov.au/nla.news-article158106299.

The White Squall: Barker, George.*The white squall : sea song.* French Musical Instrument Depot, Sydney 1880. Accessed July 25, 2016. http://nla.gov.au/nla.obj-168033811/view#page/n0/mode/1up.

Destitute

Destitute Asylum and Destitute Board: Painter, Alison. "19 March 1849 Destitute Asylum." *SA 175 (Professional Historians Association (SA).* Accessed December 31, 2015. http://www.sahistorians.org.au/175/chronology/march/19-march-184 9-destitute-asylum.shtml.

Geyer, Mary Louise. "Destitute Asylum | Adelaidia." *Adelaidia.* Accessed October 11, 2016. http://adelaidia.sa.gov.au/places/destitute-asylum.

Piddock, Susan. *Accommodating the Destitute: An Historical and Archaeological Consideration of the Destitute Asylum of Adelaide.* Flinders University of South Australia, 1996. Chapter 2 viewed online at https://www.researchgate.net/publication/306016897_Accommodati ng_the_Destitute_Chapter_2

John Mason's application to Destitute Board: Minutes of Destitute Board of South Australia 1849-1927, GRG 28/1, Item No 674 'Jno. Mason.'. State Records of South Australia, Adelaide. Cited 24 November 2015.

John's death: John Mason, death certificate (22 January 1857), South Australian Register of Births Deaths and Marriages. Transcription provided by SA Genealogy & Heraldry Society.

John's Death notice: "Advertising" *South Australian Register,* 23 Jan 1857. Trove. http://nla.gov.au/nla.news-article49768656.

Nature of rations provided by Destitute Board: "GOVERNMENT GAZETTE NOTICES" *Adelaide Observer* 23 Nov 1850. Trove. http://nla.gov.au/nla.news-article159532542.

Catherine's applications to the Destitute Board: "DESTITUTE BOARD. - MONDAY, JUNE 1." *South Australian Register,* 2 Jun 1857.

"DESTITUTE BOARD. MONDAY, JANUARY 4." *Adelaide Observer,* January 9, 1858.

"DESTITUTE BOARD. - MONDAY, MARCH 1." *Adelaide Times*, 2 Mar 1858.

"DESTITUTE BOARD. - MONDAY, AUGUST 22." *The South Australian Advertiser,* 24 Aug 1859.

"DESTITUTE BOARD. - MONDAY, NOVEMBER 28." *The South Australian Advertiser,*29 Nov 1859. All accessed on Trove.

Life on the streets

Mason family marriages: Ancestry.com. *Australia, Marriage Index, 1788-1950.* Rose listed as Rosanna.

Births to Mason daughters: Ancestry.com. Australia, *Birth Index, 1788-1922.* Catherine Mason listed as Katherine on some entries.

Henry Atkin's court appearances: "POLICE COURT—ADELAIDE. - MONDAY, DECEMBER 14. [Before Mr. S. Beddome. P.M.]" *The South Australian Advertiser,* 15 Dec 1863. Trove. http://nla.gov.au/nla.news-article31831014.

"POLICE COURT.—ADELAIDE. - September 26. Tuesday:. (Before Messrs. S. Beddome, P.M.. and Dr. Ward.)" *The South Australian Advertiser.* 28 Sep 1865. Trove. http://nla.gov.au/nla.news-article31853995.

Irish taboo on premarital sex: Thomas Keneally, *The Great Shame: A Story of the Irish in the Old World and the New,* (Random House Australia, 1999), 4-5.

Branding of deserters: Simon Barnard, *Convict Tattoos: Marked Men and Women of Australia,* (Text Publishing, 2016), 54-55

Soldier's accommodation in Adelaide: "THE BARRACKS." *Adelaide Observer*, 9 Feb 1867. Trove. http://nla.gov.au/nla.news-article159508393.

Susan in court 1867: "POLICE COURTS. - ADELAIDE: TUESDAY, DECEMBER 10. [Before Mr. S. Beddome, P.M.]" *South Australian Register.* 11 Dec 1867. Trove. http://nla.gov.au/nla.news-article39179657.

Susan Cavanagh: "POLICE COURT—PORT ADELAIDE. FRIDAY, JUNE 3. [Before Mr. R. F. Newland.]." *The South Australian Advertiser.* 4 June 1859. Trove. http://nla.gov.au/nla.news-article793689

"POLICE COURTS. ADELAIDE: FRIDAY, MARCH 28. [Before Mr. S. Beddome. P.M.]." *South Australian Register.* 29 Mar. 1862. Trove. http://trove.nla.gov.au/newspaper/article/40470259.

"PORT ADELAIDE: FRIDAY, AUGUST 14 [Before Mr. G. W. Hawkes, S.M.]." *Adelaide Observer*. August 15, 1863. Trove. http://nla.gov.au/nla.news-article159519493.

"POLICE COURTS. ADELAIDE: SATURDAY, APRIL 17. [Before Mr. S. Beddome. P.M.]." *Adelaide Observer*. April 24, 1869. Trove. http://nla.gov.au/nla.news-article158937025.

Alice Freer: "LOCAL COURT—GAWLER. TUESDAY, NOVEMBER 22. [Before Mr. R. J. Turner S.m.]." *The Adelaide Express*. November 23, 1864. Trove. http://nla.gov.au/nla.news-article207597640.

"LAW COURTS. - POLICE COURT—ADELAIDE. THIS DAY. SATURDAY, JUNE 16. [Before Mr. S. Beddome, P.M.]". *The Adelaide Express.* 16 Jun 1866. Trove. http://nla.gov.au/nla.news-article207608749.

Ann Connor: "A PAIR OF IRISH RUFFIANS." *The Wallaroo Times and Mining Journal.* 6 May 1865. Trove. http://nla.gov.au/nla.news-article110099465.

Irish female immigrants: Marie Ann Steiner, *Servants Depots in Colonial South Australia*, (Wakefield Press, 2009), 3-8.

C. W. Parkin, "Irish Female Immigration to South Australia during the Great Famine", Adelaide 1964. Thesis (B.A.Hons.), University of Adelaide.

Trevor McLaughlin in *The Irish Women's History Reader*, Edited Alan Hayes and Diane Urquhart, Psychology Press, 2001, chapter 23. Taken from *Barefoot and Pregnant - Irish Famine Orphans in Australia*, Melbourne, 1991.

Soldiers' riot of 1847: "LOCAL INTELLIGENCE." South Australian Register. January 20, 1847. Trove. http://trove.nla.gov.au/newspaper/article/48543404.

Fear of Russian Invasion: quoted from Geoffrey Manning, *"The Russians are Coming - The Defence of Colonial South Australia"*, unpublished manuscript, in "Defence of the Colony.", State Library of South Australia website. Accessed October 14, 2016. http://www.slsa.sa.gov.au/manning/sa/defence/defence.htm.

Arrival of 50th regiment in SA: "DISTRIBUTION OF TROOPS." *South Australian Register*. June 19, 1867. Trove. http://nla.gov.au/nla.news-article39190584.

"SHIPPING NEWS. - ARRIVED. FRIDAY, AUGUST 9." *South Australian Weekly Chronicle,* 10 Aug 1867." Trove. http://nla.gov.au/nla.news-article91263751.

Irish soldiers in British army: Karsten, Peter. "Irish Soldiers in the British Army, 1792-1922: Suborned or Subordinate?" *Journal of Social History* 17, no. 1 (1983): 31-64. http://www.jstor.org/stable/3787238

David's birth: "FreeBMD. England & Wales, FreeBMD Birth Index, 1837-1915 Ancestry.com , accessed 4 August 2012; citing General Register Office. England and Wales Civil Registration Indexes. London, England.

James' death: Findmypast.com. *National Burial Index*. Original source: burial record from All Saints Church, Wakes Colne, Essex.

Sarah's death: FindMyPast.com, *National Burial Index*.

David's residence in workhouse: Ancestry.com: *1851 census, England*, Class: HO107; Piece: 1782; Folio: 472; Page: 20; item David Whybrew; digital image.

Workhouse children's education: *British Farmer's Magazine*. James Ridgway, 1851, 174. Letter reprinted from The Morning Chronicle.

David's enlistment and army records: FindMyPast.com. *Chelsea Pensioner Images*, digital images. Indexed as David Whybrow, birth parish Warminster. Original source: TNA UK, WO97, Box 1962, Box record number 226.

Army discipline: Peter Burroughs, "Crime and Punishment in the British Army, 1815-1870", *The English Historical Review* vol 100, no. 396 (Jul 1985): 545-571.

Adelaide Royal visit:"THE ROYAL VISIT. THE REVIEW." *South Australian Register*. November 4, 1867. Trove.

A girl of such a character

The first hearing of the case: "POLICE COURTS. ADELAIDE: SATURDAY, APRIL 11. [Before Mr. S. Beddome.P.M.]." *Adelaide Observer*. April 18, 1868. Trove.
http://trove.nla.gov.au/newspaper/article/158930525

Supreme Court hearing: "LAW AND CRIMINAL COURTS. SUPREME COURT.—CRIMINAL SITTINGS. Tuesday, May 19. [Before Mr. Justice Wearing.] FORGERY." *South Australian Register*. May 20, 1868.
Trove.http://trove.nla.gov.au/newspaper/article/39185417

"LAW AND CRIMINAL COURTS. SUPREME COURT—CRIMINAL SITTINGS. - TUESDAY, MAY 19. [Before Mr Justice Wearing.] FORGERY." *Adelaide Observer,* 23 May 1868. Trove. http://nla.gov.au/nla.news-article158931258.

"LAW COURTS, SUPREME COURT—CRIMINAL SITTINGS. (Concluded from Yesterday.) LARCENY FROM THE PERSON." *The Express and Telegraph.* May 20, 1868. Trove. http://nla.gov.au/nla.news-article207738435.

"LAW COURTS. SUPREME COURT—CRIMINAL SITTINGS. Tuesday, Mat IS. [Before His Honor Mr. Justice Wearing.]." *The South Australian Advertiser*. May 20, 1868. Trove. http://nla.gov.au/nla.news-article31978326.

Motherhood and marriage

Harriet's birth: Ancestry.com. *Australia, Birth Index, 1788-1922.* Indexed as Harriet Whybrow.

19th century childbirth: Margaret Anderson, History SA, "19th Century Childbirth", SA History Hub, History SA, accessed 17 October 2016.
http://sahistoryhub.com.au/subjects/19th-century-childbirth.

St Joseph's Refuge, Franklin Street: Find & Connect Web Resource Project, The University of Melbourne and Australian Catholic University. "St Joseph's Refuge - Organisation - Find & Connect - South Australia." Document. Accessed October 17, 2016.
https://www.findandconnect.gov.au/ref/sa/biogs/SE00042b.htm.

Destitute Persons Relief Act: "Destitute Persons Relief Act 1866 - Summary | Find & Connect." Accessed October 17, 2016.
https://www.findandconnect.gov.au/guide/sa/SE00359.

Baby farming: "BABY-FARMING." *The Irish Harp and Farmers' Herald,* 25 Apr 1873. Trove. Accessed October 17, 2016.
http://nla.gov.au/nla.news-article224364688.

"BABY FARMING." *South Australian Weekly Chronicle,* 18 Feb 1882. Accessed Trove October 18, 2016.
http://nla.gov.au/nla.news-article91290367.

Harriet's care: Circumstantial evidence suggests that Susan did not breast-feed Harriet for any length of time, if at all. Most women in this era gave birth to their children about two years apart, due mainly to the contraceptive effect of breast feeding. Susan became pregnant again within three or four months of Harriet's birth.

F W Lindrum obituary: "OBITUARY." *South Australian Register,* 7 Feb 1880. Trove.
http://nla.gov.au/nla.news-article43101144.

Announcement of 50th regiment's departure: "HOSPITAL REGULATIONS". *South Australian Register.* 25 May 1868. Trove.
http://nla.gov.au/nla.news-article39185123.

"THE AGRICULTURAL AREAS TRIUMPHANT." *South Australian Register.* 23 Dec 1868. Trove. http://nla.gov.au/nla.news-article41393752.

British Army attitudes to marriage: Venning, Annabel. *Following the Drum.* Headline review, 2006, 12-14.

Strachan, Hew. *The British Army, Manpower, and Society Into the Twenty-First Century.* Taylor & Francis, 2000. 87-89

On and off the strength: ibid, p90.

Trustram, Myna. *Women of the Regiment: Marriage and the Victorian Army.* Cambridge University Press, 1984. p31

Departure of the troops:
"MILITARY AND VOLUNTEER INTELLIGENCE." *South Australian Register.* April 24, 1869. Trove http://nla.gov.au/nla.news-article4138964

David in hiding: Ancestry.com. *South Australia, Australia, Police Gazettes, 1862-1947.* Original data from South Australia Police Gazette Indexes, 1862-1947. Ridgehaven, South Australia: Gould Genealogy and History, 2009.

50th regiment deserters:"THE WEEK'S NEWS". *Adelaide Observer.* 10 Apr 1869. Trove. http://nla.gov.au/nla.news-article158936756.

Susan and David's marriage: Transcript of South Australian District Marriage Certificate for David Whybrew and Susan Mason, 1869. Transcribed by Genealogy SA.

David's trial for desertion:"POLICE COURT—ADELAIDE. THIS DAY, TUESDAY, JUNE 8. [Before Mr. S. Beddome, P.M.]." *The Express and Telegraph.* June 8, 1869. Trove http://nla.gov.au/nla.news-article207742941

Third child conceived: It may be, of course, that Susan had one or more unrecorded miscarriages in this period.

The army wife

Conditions on board ship:"1850s–70s: a long and dangerous journey". Museum Victoria. Accessed November 22, 2016. https://museumvictoria.com.au/discoverycentre/websites-mini/journeys-australia/1850s70s/.

Susan in Aldershot: Ancestry.com. *1871 England Census.* Original source: *Census Returns of England and Wales, 1871.* TNA UK: Public Record Office (PRO), 1871. Class: RG10; Piece: 817; Folio: 16; Page: 28; GSU roll: 827758

Henry Hudson's army records: Ancestry.com. UK, *Royal Hospital Chelsea Pensioner Admissions and Discharges, 1715-1925.* Original source: *Royal Hospital, Chelsea: Disability and Royal Artillery Out-Pensions, Admission Books*; Class: WO 116; Piece Number: 107.

Life for army wives "on the strength": Bamfield, Veronica. *On the Strength: The Story of the British Army Wife.* C. Knight, 1974.

"Soldiers Wives." *Edinburgh Evening News.* May 28, 1875, p4. BLNA.

Cardwell reforms: Strachan, Hew. *The British Army, Manpower, and Society Into the Twenty-First Century.* Taylor & Francis, 2000. p90.

Marriage and the plight of army wives "off the strength": "HOW OUR SOLDIERS WIVES AND CHILDREN ARE KEPT" *Morning Advertiser.* April 1, 1871.p3 BLNA.

"Autumn Assizes at Beford",*Luton Times and Advertiser.* 31 October, 1879. p8. BLNA.

Communication with Adelaide: Adelaide was first connected to the rest of the world via a link through Darwin and Java in August 1872. This was such a momentous event that it was marked with a public holiday. At £9 per twenty words, the cost of a telegram was well outside the ordinary person's reach.

Rosina Whybrew's birth: FreeBMD. England & Wales, *Civil Registration Birth Index, 1837-1915.* Listed as "Rosina Whybruew".

Original data: GRO. *England and Wales Civil Registration Indexes*. London, England: GRO. Essex, vol 4a p 326.

David Whybrew junior's death: GRO death certificate. Indexed at Colchester, 1874, vol 4a, entry 169.

Captain Fleury's marriage: "Family Notices" *South Australian Register*. 7 Nov 1868. Trove. http://nla.gov.au/nla.news-article41400723.

Arrival in Dublin: "Military Intelligence. *Freemans Journal*. Saturday August 8 1874. BLNA.

Rosina's death: Ireland Register Office death certificate. Indexed South Dublin, October 1874, entry 40. Indexed as Rose Whybren.

Dublin whiskey fire: "IRELAND. - DESTRUCTIVE FIRE IN DUBLIN." *Australian Town and Country Journal*. 31 July, 1875. Trove. http://nla.gov.au/nla.news-article70584224.

Movements of the 50th regiment: Fyler, Arthur Evelyn. *The History of the 50th Or (the Queen's Own) Regiment from the Earliest Date*. Chapman and Hall, 1895. Appendix IX http://archive.org/details/historythorquee00fylegoog

Bridget Lyon case: "County Intelligence", *Whitstable Times and Herne Bay Herald*. 16 August 1879. p3. BLNA.

Foggarty case: "COUNTY INTELLIGENCE CANTERBURY". *Whitstable Times and Herne Bay Herald*. 24 July 1880, p2.

1881 census in Dover: Ancestry.com. Original source: *Census Returns of England and Wales, 1881*. TNA UK: Public Record Office (PRO), 1881.Class: RG11; Piece: 1004; Folio: 60; Page: 11; GSU roll: 1341238. Indexed as "Susan Wibram".

Rose Morris death: "Family Notices" *South Australian Register*. 5 Jun 1878. Accessed Trove, November 28, 2016. http://nla.gov.au/nla.news-article42988886.

Margaret Atkin death: "Family Notices." *South Australian Register*. May 3, 1879. Trove. http://nla.gov.au/nla.news-article42976220 .

Jane Mason's illness and death: South Australian Government Archives, GRG 78/49 *Royal Adelaide Hospital Admissions 1840-1904* M-R http://www.archives.sa.gov.au/content/admission-registers Unley Libraries Family history transcription service, South Australian register of deaths, packet no 97 fiche no 6.

Sittingbourne skulls: "Sittingbourne".*The Whitstable Times and Herne Bay Herald.* Saturday, May 23, 1885; p3; Issue 1116.BLNA.

Reunion and conflict

F. W. Lindrum obituary: "OBITUARY". *South Australian Register.* 7 Feb 1880. Trove.
http://nla.gov.au/nla.news-article43101144.

Clara Lindrum insolvency: "LAW COURTS. INSOLVENCY COURT. - APPOINTMENTS. TUESDAY, NOVEMBER 15". *The Express and Telegraph* 12 Nov 1881. Trove.
http://nla.gov.au/nla.news-article208196797.

"INSOLVENCY COURT. - APPOINTMENTS. TUESDAY, DECEMBER 13". *The Express and Telegraph.* 12 Dec 1881. Trove.
http://nla.gov.au/nla.news-article208198050.

"Advertising". *The Express and Telegraph,* 23 Nov 1881. Trove.
http://nla.gov.au/nla.news-article208197248.

Harriet's 1882 court appearance: "TUESDAY, JANUARY 17. - [Before Mr. S. Beddome, P.M.]" *South Australian Weekly Chronicle.* 21 Jan 1882. Trove. http://nla.gov.au/nla.news-article91290505.

Industrial school Magill: "INDUSTRIAL SCHOOLS. - TO THE EDITOR". *Adelaide Observer.* 14 Apr 1883. Trove.
http://nla.gov.au/nla.news-article159561021.

"DESTITUTE COMMISSION." *Adelaide Observer.* 10 May 1884. Trove. http://nla.gov.au/nla.news-article160096227.

Find & Connect Web Resource Project, The University of Melbourne and Australian Catholic University. "Girls Reformatory, Magill - Organisation - Find & Connect - South Australia." Document. Accessed November 29, 2016.
http://www.findandconnect.gov.au/ref/sa/biogs/SE00066b.htm.

Harriet's admission to Industrial school: State Archives of South Australia, "Register of Admissions - Destitute Asylum" GRG 28/5, record id 45/1882.

Riotous behaviour in May: "POLICE COURT-ADELAIDE. WEDNESDAY, MAY 3. [Before Mr. S. Beddome, P.M.]." *The Express and Telegraph.* May 4, 1882. p2. Trove.
http://nla.gov.au/nla.news-article208258588

Back in court in October 1882:"POLICE COURTS. ADELAIDE: MONDAY OCTOBER 16. [Before Messrs. S. Beddome, P.M., H. Fraser, and Curnow, J.P.'s.]." *Adelaide Observer.* October 28, 1882. P2. Trove. http://trove.nla.gov.au/newspaper/article/160163122

Last Adelaide court appearance 1885:"POLICE COURT—ADELAIDE. - THIS DAY. THURSDAY, AUGUST 20. [Before Mr. S. Beddome, P.M., the Hon. S. Tomkinson, M.L.C., and Mr. J. Williams.]" *The Express and Telegraph* 20 Aug 1885. Trove. http://nla.gov.au/nla.news-article208353081.

Life of a laundress: see https://clogsandclippers.blogspot.com.au/2016/09/the-life-of-laundre ss.html

David charged with assault: "Colchester Borough". *Essex Standard.* 18 August 1888 p2. BLNA.

Susan charged with assault: "Colchester Borough Oct 18". *Essex Standard.* 20 October 1888 p8. BLNA.

1853 Act: "The Act for the Better Prevention and Punishment of Aggravated Assaults upon Women and Children." See http://www.legislation.gov.uk/ukpga/Vict/16-17/30/enacted

Separation and divorce: Helena Wojtczak. "British Women's Emancipation since the Renaissance." History of Women website. Accessed December 2, 2016. http://www.historyofwomen.org/wifebeating.html

Harriet in court 1890: "Colchester (Borough) Oct 27". Essex County *Chronicle.* 31 October 1890 p2.BLNA.

The end of an era

Mr Beddome retirement: "LETTERS TO PUBLIC MEN. - SAMUEL BEDDOME, POLICE MAGISTRATE. *Quiz.* 31 Jan 1890. Trove. http://nla.gov.au/nla.news-article166370024.

"RETIREMENT OF MR. S BEDDOME, S.M. - REMINISCENCES OF THE ADELAIDE POLICE COURT". *South Australian Register.* 26 Jul 1890. Trove. http://nla.gov.au/nla.news-article47283719.

Mr Beddome's son's suicide: "SUICIDE OF MB. H. L BEDDOME. - THE INQUEST." *Evening Journal.* 24 Mar 1890. Trove. http://nla.gov.au/nla.news-article207196490.

Ellen Whybrew's birth: FreeBMD.org.uk Births, Whybrew, Ellen, 1890 Q1, Colchester, vol 4a, p 570 (not indexed on Ancestry.com.)

Henry Malone: "India Births and Baptisms, 1786-1947," database, FS. FHL microfilm 521,856. https://familysearch.org/ark:/61903/1:1:FGHS-J9N : 8 December 2014. Information about Henry's childhood experience is based on 1871, 1881 UK census records.

David's accident: "COLCHESTER".*The Essex Standard, West Suffolk Gazette, and Eastern Counties' Advertiser.* Saturday, March 14, 1891; p. 8; Issue 3144.BLNA

Beales family involvement in Salvation Army: personal communication with descendants.

Colchester skating rink: "Colchester -Its Contribution to the History of The Skating Rink." Colchesteruncovered.wordpress.com, May 30, 2014. https://colchesteruncovered.wordpress.com/2014/05/30/datatextmce-internalcolchester-its-contribution-to-the-history-of-the-skating-rink/.

Opposition to Salvation army in Colchester: "News".*Essex Halfpenny Newsman*(Chelmsford, England), Saturday, October 01, 1881; p. 3; Issue 595.BLNA.

Salvation Army in South Australia: THQ, The Salvation Army Australia Eastern Territory. "Australian Beginnings Salvos.org.au/emerald/." https://salvos.org.au/emerald/our-history/australian-beginnings/.

Patricia Sumerling. "The West End of Adelaide 1870-1936." *Professional Historians Association*, http://www.sahistorians.org.au/175/bm.doc/sumerling-west-end-4.doc.

"WITH SALVATION SOLDIERS AND HALLELUJAH LASSES. - [BY A SPECIAL.]" *Evening Journal.* 5 May 1883. Trove. http://nla.gov.au/nla.news-article197785671.

Susan vs Harriet Kettle 1892: "COLCHESTER POLICE COURTS". *The Essex Standard, West Suffolk Gazette, and Eastern Counties' Advertiser*), Saturday, June 11, 1892; p. 7; Issue 3209. BLNA.

Susan vs Rose Belfall 1895: "COLCHESTER POLICE COURTS".*The Essex County Standard West Suffolk Gazette, and Eastern Counties Advertiser*), Saturday, April 06, 1895; p. 3; Issue 3356.BLNA.

Susan vs Annie Jukes 1900: "Petty Sessions".*Essex Newsman*, Saturday, November 17, 1900; p. 2; Issue 1609.BLNA.

John Whybrew's military records: TNA UK. *Royal Hospital Chelsea: Soldiers Service Documents*; Series: WO 97; Piece Number: 4158. John's regimental number was 4692.

Ancestry.com. UK, *Silver War Badge Records, 1914-1920*. Original data: *War Office and Air Ministry: Service Medal and Award Rolls, First World War*. Silver War Badge. RG WO 329, 2958–3255. TNA UK.

Henry Whybrew's military records: Ancestry.com. *British Army WWI Service Records, 1914-1920*. (Henry's Boer War service has been misfiled on the site under "Henry Whybrow", WW1, but the images clearly show Henry's records from enlistment in 1898 to his death in 1902, including his parent's names.)Original data: TNA UK: Public Record Office (PRO). Regimental number 6727.

Susan vs Annie Jukes: "Petty Sessions".*Essex Newsman*, Saturday, November 17, 1900; p. 2; Issue 1609.BLNA.

Deaths of Eliza and Jeremiah Murphy: personal communication from Nigel Cooper

The Boer War: "Second Boer War." *Wikipedia*, December 4, 2016.

https://en.wikipedia.org/w/index.php?title=Second_Boer_War&oldid=753005787.

Henry's death: Ancestry.com. *UK, Army Registers of Soldiers' Effects, 1901-1929*. Original source: National Army Museum; Chelsea, London, England; *Soldiers' Effects Records, 1901-60*; NAM Accession Number: 1991-02-333; Record Number Ranges: 88001-89470; Reference: 32

Ancestry.com. *Casualties of the Boer War, 1899-1902*. Original data: Military-Genealogy.com, comp. Boer War Casualties 1899-1902. The Naval and Military Press Ltd. www.military-genealogy.com.

Henry's grave at Springfontein: Genealogical Society of South Africa virtual branch http://www.eggsa.org/library/main.php?g2_itemId=712864

Herbert Miller's migration: "Canada Passenger Lists, 1881-1922," database with images, *FS* (https://familysearch.org/ark:/61903/1:1:2QS4-F67 : 27 December 2014), H A Miller, Apr 1905; citing Immigration, Halifax, Nova Scotia, Canada, T-499, Library and Archives Canada, Ottawa, Ontario.

Alice Whybrew Miller's migration: Canada, Library and Archives. "Image: Passenger Lists for the Port of Quebec City and Other Ports, 1865-1922," May 31, 2013. http://www.bac-lac.gc.ca/eng/discover/immigration/immigration-rec ords/passenger-lists/passenger-lists-quebec-port-1865-1900/Pages/im age.aspx?Image=e003658577&URLjpg=http://central.bac-lac.gc.ca/. item/?id=e003658577&op=img&Ecopy=e003658577.

Alice Frances Miller's immigration record: "Michigan, Detroit Manifests of Arrivals at the Port of Detroit, 1906-1954," database with images, *FS* (https://familysearch.org/ark:/61903/1:1:K8MS-S5D), Alice Frances Miller, 12 Jul 1906; citing NARA microfilm publication M1478 (Washington, D.C.: National Archives and Records Administration, n.d.); FHL microfilm 1,490,512.

William Whybrew's marriage: details from marriage certificate: GRO, *England and Wales Civil Registration Indexes*. London, England: GRO. Essex, vol 4a, p 1392

Susan vs James McBirnie: "Petty Sessions".*Essex Newsman*, Saturday, August 05, 1905; p. 2; Issue 1856.BLNA.

Rose and George's travel to USA: "Canada Passenger Lists, 1881-1922," database with images, *FS* (https://familysearch.org/ark:/61903/1:1:2Q3N-G7R : 27 December 2014), Rose Anthony, Jun 1907; citing Immigration, Quebec City, Quebec, Canada, T-490, Library and Archives Canada, Ottawa, Ontario.

"Vermont, St. Albans Canadian Border Crossings, 1895-1954," database with images, *FS* (https://familysearch.org/ark:/61903/1:1:QK3B-21ZV : 9 October 2015), Rose Anthony, 1895-1924; citing M1461, Soundex Index to Canadian Border Entries through the St. Albans, Vermont, District, 1895-1924, 12, NARA microfilm publications M1461, M1463, M1464, and M1465 (Washington D.C.: National Archives and Records Administration, publication year); FHL microfilm 1,472,812.

Alice Whybrew Miller's death: "Illinois, Cook County Deaths, 1878-1994," database, *FS* (https://familysearch.org/ark:/61903/1:1:Q2MQ-X8ZT : 17 May 2016), Alice Miller, 07 Dec 1909; citing Chicago, Cook, Illinois, United States, source reference 29077, record number , Cook County Courthouse, Chicago; FHL microfilm 1,239,844.

Herbert Miller's marriage to Alice McKeon: "Illinois, Cook County Marriages, 1871-1920," database, *FS* (https://familysearch.org/ark:/61903/1:1:N7CQ-SQN : 26 December 2014), Herbert A. Miller and Alice M. Mckeon, 12 Mar 1910; citing Chicago, Cook, Illinois, 529686, Cook County Courthouse, Chicago; FHL microfilm 1,030,474.

Susan and David in 1911 UK census: Ancestry.com. *1911 England Census*. Original data: Census Returns of England and Wales, 1911. TNA UK, 1911. Class: RG14; Piece: 10291; Schedule Number: 15.

Death of young George Anthony: "Illinois, Cook County Deaths, 1878-1994," database, *FS* (https://familysearch.org/ark:/61903/1:1:Q2M7-P8NP : 17 May 2016), George Anthony in entry for George W Anthony, 30 Apr 1913; citing Chicago, Cook, Illinois, United States, source reference 16512, record number , Cook County Courthouse, Chicago; FHL microfilm 1,287,643.

George Anthony senior's draft registration card: "United States World War I Draft Registration Cards, 1917-1918," database with images, *FS* (https://familysearch.org/ark:/61903/1:1:K68B-X9T : 12 December 2014), George Anthony, 1917-1918; citing Chicago City no 86, Illinois, United States, NARA microfilm publication

M1509 (Washington D.C.: National Archives and Records Administration, n.d.); FHL microfilm 1,504,081.

George Anthony sen. Possible death: "Illinois Deaths and Stillbirths, 1916-1947," database, *FS* (https://familysearch.org/ark:/61903/1:1:N3ZH-89D : 27 December 2014), George Anthony, 16 May 1941; Public Board of Health, Archives, Springfield; FHL microfilm 1,832,584.

Exhaustion

Voluntary Aid Detachments: "Voluntary Aid Detachment." *Wikipedia*, November 4, 2016. https://en.wikipedia.org/w/index.php?title=Voluntary_Aid_Detachment&oldid=747779044.

Short war expected: Tuchman, Barbara Wertheim. *The Guns of August*. Ballantine, 2004. p140-142

John Whybrew's possible enlistment 1914: Ancestry.com. *British Army WWI Medal Rolls Index Cards, 1914-1920* [database on-line]. Provo, UT, USA: Ancestry.com Operations Inc, 2008. John Whybrew, regiment number SE/510. Original data: Army Medal Office. WWI Medal Index Cards. In the care of The Western Front Association website.

William Whybrew's army records: Ancestry.com. UK, *WWI Service Medal and Award Rolls, 1914-1920*. Original source: TNA UK. *WWI Service Medal and Award Rolls;* Class: WO 329; Piece Number: 956. William Whybrew, regimental number 34021.

Ancestry.com. *UK, Army Registers of Soldiers' Effects, 1901-1929*. Original source: National Army Museum; Chelsea, London, England; *Soldiers' Effects Records, 1901-60;* NAM Accession Number: 1991-02-333; Record Number Ranges: 844001-845500; Reference: 514. William Whybrew, Yorkshire Regiment, regimental number 34021.

William and Adelaide (Annie) in UK Census 1911: Ancestry.com. *1911 England Census*. Original data: *Census Returns of England and Wales, 1911*. TNA UK, 1911. Class: RG14; Piece: 9105; Schedule Number: 158

Henry Lawrence connection: Ancestry.com. *British Army WWI Pension Records 1914-1920*. Original data: TNA UK. WO364; Piece: 2055

Bomb dropped on Colchester: "Plaque Recognises WW1 Bomb Attack." *Gazette*. Accessed March 3, 2016.

http://www.gazette-news.co.uk/news/11816968.Plaque_recognises_
WW1_bomb_attack/.

Pathé, British. "House At Colchester Damaged."
http://www.britishpathe.com/video/house-at-colchester-damaged/que
ry/bombs.

Conditions in Colchester: Read, Julian. "Colchester Memories."
Essex Life. Story contributed by Albert Bridges.
http://www.essexlifemag.co.uk/out-about/places/colchester_memorie
s_1_3588763.

Army form B104-82: "British Soldiers Who Died in the War
1914-1918." The Long Long Trail.
http://www.1914-1918.net/died.htm.

George Howard's death: Ancestry.com. UK, *Army Registers of
Soldiers' Effects, 1901-1929.* Original source: National Army
Museum; Chelsea, London, England; *Soldiers' Effects Records,
1901-60;* NAM Accession Number: 1991-02-333; Record Number
Ranges: 544001-545500; Reference: 315.

See also Stotfold Roll of Honour:
http://www.roll-of-honour.com/Bedfordshire/StotfoldRollofHonour.
html

William Whybrew's death: Military-Genealogy.com, comp.
UK, *Soldiers Died in the Great War, 1914-1919* Original data: *British
and Irish Military Databases*. The Naval and Military Press Ltd.

Ipswich War Memorial: Memorial, Ipswich War. "WILLIAM
WHYBREW." *Ipswich War Memorial*, June 29, 2016.
http://www.ipswichwarmemorial.co.uk/william-whybrew/.

Yorkshire regiment deaths: "The Yorkshire Regiment, WW1
Remembrance - Introduction."
http://www.ww1-yorkshires.org.uk/html-files/introduction.htm.

David Whybrew's death: details from death certificate. GRO.
England and Wales Civil Registration Indexes. London, England:
GRO. Essex vol 4a p 725

David's burial: Colchester cemetery plot L.11.15. Details
supplied by staff at Colchester Cemetery.

Third Anglo-Afghan War: the background to this brief conflict
was complex, but essentially it came about as a result of Afghanistan's
move towards independence from Britain during and after the First
World War, and Britain's concern that Russia might seek greater
influence in Afghanistan. See
https://www.britannica.com/event/Third-Anglo-Afghan-War.

Susan's move to Campion Rd: detail from death certificate.

Susan's death: Details from death certificate. GRO. *England and Wales Civil Registration Indexes*. London, England: GRO. Essex, vol 4a p 791

Susan's burial: Colchester Cemetery plot L.11.16. Details supplied by Colchester Cemetery staff.

Bibliography

Books

Ancient Order of Foresters Friendly Society, Adelaide District, 1870-1872: Court Perseverance No. 2221, Established May, 1847, Held at the Norfolk Arms, Rundle Street. Bro. Shawyer, 1870.

Australia. Parliament. Joint Library Committee, and Frederick Watson. *Historical Records of Australia*. Sydney : The Library Committee of the Commonwealth Parliament, 1923. http://archive.org/details/historicalrecord00v17aust.

Bamfield, Veronica. *On the Strength: The Story of the British Army Wife*. C. Knight, 1974.

Barnard, Simon. *Convict Tattoos: Marked Men and Women of Australia*. Text Publishing, 2016.

Bennett, James F. *Historical and Descriptive Account of South Australia: Founded on the Experience of a Three Years' Residence in That Colony*. Smith, Elder & Company, 1843.

British Farmer's Magazine. James Ridgway, 1851.

Chauncy, W. Snell. *A Guide to South Australia: Being a Descriptive Account of the Colony; Addressed to Intending Emigrants, and Containing the Latest Authentic Information*. Public Library of South Australia, 1849.

Commons, Great Britain Parliament House of. *Parliamentary Papers, House of Commons and Command*. H.M. Stationery Office, 1838.

Duncan, Beth. *Mary Thomas: Founding Mother: The Life and Times of a South Australian Pioneer*. Kent Town, S. Aust: Wakefield Press, 2007.

Foster, Robert, and Paul Sendziuk, eds. *Turning Points: Chapters in South Australian History*. Wakefield Press, 2012.

Frederick Sinnett. *An Account of the Colony of South Australia Prepared for Distribution at the International Exhibition of 1862 / by Frederick Sinnett. Together with a Catalogue of All the Products of South Australia Exhibited in the South Australian Court of the International Exhibition*. London: Robert K. Burt, 1862.

Fyler, Arthur Evelyn . *The History of the 50th Or (the Queen's Own) Regiment from the Earliest Date ...* Chapman and Hall, 1895. http://archive.org/details/historythorquee00fylegoog.

Garran, Andrew. *The Royal South Australian Book Almanack and General Directory, for 1854: Calculated for the Meridian of Adelaide.* "Register" and "Observer" Office, 1854.

General Laws of the South Australian Ancient Order of Foresters Friendly Society: Being the Ancient Order of Foresters, Adelaide District, Established Under the District Dispensation Granted by the High Court in England of the Ancient Order of Foresters in the Year 1847, 1907.

Harrison, Robert. *Colonial Sketches: Or, Five Years in South Australia, with Hints to Capitalists and Emigrants.* Hall, Virtue, 1862.

Hayes, Alan, and Diane Urquhart. *The Irish Women's History Reader.* Psychology Press, 2001.

Keneally, Thomas. *The Great Shame: A Story of the Irish in the Old World and the New.* Random House Australia, 1999.

Lewis, Milton James. *The People's Health: Public Health in Australia, 1788-1950.* Greenwood Publishing Group, 2003.

MacKenzie, Rev David. *Ten Years in Australia ..: With an Introductory Chapter Containing the Latest Information Regarding the Colony.* William S. Orr and Co., 1851.

Malcolmson, Patricia E. *English Laundresses: A Social History, 1850-1930.* University of Illinois Press, 1986.

"McLaren, David (1785–1850)." In *Australian Dictionary of Biography.* Canberra: National Centre of Biography, Australian National University. Accessed June 3, 2016. http://adb.anu.edu.au/biography/mclaren-david-2412.

Nicholas, Stephen. *Convict Workers: Reinterpreting Australia's Past.* Cambridge University Press, 1988.

Oram, Hugh. *Bygone Limerick: The City and County in Days Gone by.* Mercier Press Ltd, 2010.

Piddock, Susan. *Accommodating the Destitute: An Historical and Archaeological Consideration of the Destitute Asylum of Adelaide.* Flinders University of South Australia, 1996.

Pike, Douglas. *Paradise of Dissent: South Australia 1829-1857.* London: Longmans, Green and Co, 1957.

Proceedings of the Parliament of South Australia: With Copies of Documents Ordered to Be Printed ..., 1868.

Spiers, Edward M. *The Late Victorian Army, 1868-1902*. Manchester University Press, 1992.

Steiner, Marie Ann. *Servants Depots in Colonial South Australia*. Wakefield Press, 2009.

Strachan, Hew. *The British Army, Manpower, and Society Into the Twenty-First Century*. Taylor & Francis, 2000.

The City of Adelaide: A Thematic History. McDougall & Vines, 2006.

The Inconstant Girls: The Migration Experience of 200 Irish Orphan Girls and Young Women Sent to Adelaide in 1840 Aboard the Barque Inconstant. Lythrum Press, 2004.

The South Australian Government Gazette, 1848.

Thomas, Mary Harris. *The Diary and Letters of Mary Thomas (1836-1866): Being a Record of the Early Days of South Australia*. W.K. Thomas & Company, 1925.

Trustram, Myna. *Women of the Regiment: Marriage and the Victorian Army*. Cambridge University Press, 1984.

Tuchman, Barbara Wertheim. *The Guns of August*. Ballantine, 2004.

Venning, Annabel. *Following the Drum*. Headline review, 2006.

Wilkinson, George Blakiston. *South Australia: Its Advantages and Its Resources. Being a Description of That Colony, and a Manual of Information for Emigrants*. J. Murray, 1848.

———. *South Australia: Its Advantages and Its Resources : Being a Description of That Colony and Manual of Information for Emigrants : By George Blakiston Wilkinson*. John Murray, 1848.

———. *The Working Man's Handbook to South Australia: With Advice to the Farmer, and Detailed Information for the Several Classes of Labourers and Artizans*. J. Murray, 1849.

Articles and Documents (including on-line)

Burroughs, Peter. "Crime and Punishment in the British Army, 1815-1870." *The English Historical Review* 100, no. 396 (1985): 545–71.

"Catholic Baptisms South Australia, Adelaide District, 1841-1881"; Viewed on Microfiche, SA Genealogical Library, Unley, Adelaide, South Australia.

Dickey, Brian. "What Have Social Workers Done." Accessed December 31, 2015. www.sahistorians.org.au.

Foxhall, Katherine. "From Convicts to Colonists: The Health of Prisoners and the Voyage to Australia, 1823 – 1853." *The Journal of Imperial and Commonwealth History* 39, no. 1 (2011): 1–19. doi:10.1080/03086534.2011.543793.

Hilliard, David. "The Catholic Church in South Australia (Subpages).doc." Catholic Church of South Australia. Accessed December 29, 2015. http://www.adelaide.catholic.org.au/__files/f/8276/The%20Catholic%20Church%20in%20South%20Australia%20(sub%20pages).pdf.

Ingram, George P. "Letter to H. Tomlin," 1842.

"John Mason, South Australian District Death Certificate" (Transcript Provided by Genealogy SA). South Australian Register of Births, Deaths and Marriages, January 22, 1857.

Karsten, Peter. "Irish Soldiers in the British Army, 1792-1922: Suborned or Subordinate?" *Journal of Social History* 17, no. 1 (1983): 31–64.

McDougall, and Vines. "The City of Adelaide - a Thematic History." Adelaide City Council, 2006. http://www.adelaidecitycouncil.com/assets/acc/Council/docs/city_of_adelaide_thematic_history.pdf.

"Minutes of Destitute Board of South Australia 1849-1927, GRG 28/1, Item No 674 'Jno. Mason,'" n.d. State Records of South Australia, Adelaide, South Australia.

"New South Wales Government. Indents First Fleet, Second Fleet and Ships. State Archives NSW; Series: NRS 12189; Item: [X636]; Microfiche: 708," n.d.

Oram, Gerard. "« The Administration of Discipline by the English Is Very Rigid ». British Military Law and the Death Penalty (1868-1918)." *Crime, Histoire & Sociétés / Crime, History & Societies* 5, no. 1 (January 1, 2001): 93–110. doi:10.4000/chs.782.

Patricia Sumerling. "The West End of Adelaide 1870-1936." Professional Historians Association, n.d. http://www.sahistorians.org.au/175/bm.doc/sumerling-west-end-4.doc.

Piddock, Susan. "Accommodating the Destitute. An Historical and Archaeological Consideration of the Destitute Asylum of Adelaide." *Australian Archaeology* 0, no. 45 (1997): 63.

Red Cross. "Tommy Atkins Married." Navy & Army Illustrated, September 18, 1896. http://www.military-researcher.co.uk/Families.html.

Richards, Eric. "Irish Life and Progress in Colonial South Australia." *Irish Historical Studies* 27, no. 107 (1991): 216–36.

SLSA. "Religion : City of Churches." SLSA, December 7, 2005. http://www.samemory.sa.gov.au/site/page.cfm?u=1454.

———. "Sex Industry." SLSA, May 4, 2007. http://www.samemory.sa.gov.au/site/page.cfm?u=666.

"SRWWW Records NSW Government, Ships List, Reel 2654, [4/4780]," n.d. http://srwww.records.nsw.gov.au/ebook/list.asp?series=NRS5313&item=4_4780&ship=Navarino.

"State Records Authority of New South Wales; Copies of Deeds to Grant to Land Alienated by Grant, Lease or Purchase; Series: NRS 13836; Item: 7/507; Reel: 2705," n.d.

State Records Authority of New South Wales; Kingswood New South Wales, Australia; "Persons on Bounty Ships (Agent's Immigrant Lists); Series: 5316; Reel: 2134; Item: [4/4787]." Ancestry.com, n.d.

Unknown. "Imperial Regiments in South Australia." Charles Stuart Museum. Accessed July 26, 2016. http://www.charlessturtmuseum.com.au/resources/booklets/imperial%20regiments%20in%20south%20australia.pdf.

Websites

"19th Century Childbirth | SA History Hub." Accessed October 4, 2015. http://sahistoryhub.com.au/subjects/19th-century-childbirth.

"19th Century Cork > About Cork > - CorkCity.ie." Accessed October 5, 2015. http://www.corkcity.ie/aboutcork/historyofcork/19thcenturycork/.

"19th Century Justice - Victorian Crime and Punishment." Accessed December 2, 2016. http://vcp.e2bn.org/justice/index.php.

"1850s–70s: Museum Victoria." Accessed November 22, 2016. https://museumvictoria.com.au/discoverycentre/websites-mini/journeys-australia/1850s70s/.

Adelaide, Hindley Street 5000, and S. A. Australia. "Hindley Street Riot | Adelaidia." Accessed October 6, 2016. http://adelaidia.sa.gov.au/events/hindley-street-riot.

"Adelaide - Prostitution." *The Manning Index of South Australian History*, n.d. http://www.slsa.sa.gov.au/manning/adelaide/prosti/prosti.htm.

"Alexandra, Princess of Wales's Own (Yorkshire Regiment) ('Green Howards')." *The Long, Long Trail*. Accessed February 5, 2016. http://www.longlongtrail.co.uk/army/regiments-and-corps/the-british -infantry-regiments-of-1914-1918/alexandra-princess-of-waless-own -yorkshire-regiment-green-howards/

"Australian English; How Is It Different from British and American English?" Accessed June 20, 2016. http://www.convictcreations.com/culture/strine.htm.

"British Army during the Victorian Era." *Wikipedia, the Free Encyclopedia*, July 28, 2016. https://en.wikipedia.org/w/index.php?title=British_Army_during_the _Victorian_Era&oldid=731952091.

"British Women's Emancipation since the Renaissance." Accessed December 2, 2016. http://www.historyofwomen.org/wifebeating.html.

City of Adelaide. "Adelaide Assessment Books." Accessed October 4, 2016. http://photosau.com.au/adelaiderates/scripts/home.asp.

"Courts and Prosecution in Nineteenth Century England." Accessed March 23, 2016. http://www.bunker8.pwp.blueyonder.co.uk/history/36807.htm.

"Destitute Asylum | SA History Hub." Accessed December 31, 2015. http://sahistoryhub.com.au/places/destitute-asylum.

"Destitute Persons Relief Act 1866 - Summary | Find & Connect." Accessed October 17, 2016. https://www.findandconnect.gov.au/guide/sa/SE00359.

"Dublin Whiskey Fire." *Atlas Obscura*. Accessed March 5, 2016. http://www.atlasobscura.com/places/dublin-whiskey-fire.

"EARL GREY SCHEME." Accessed October 14, 2016. http://www.irishfaminememorial.org/history/earl-grey-scheme/.

"Fascinating Insight into the Irish Who Joined British Army | Belfast Media Group." Accessed June 7, 2016.

http://belfastmediagroup.com/fascinating-insight-into-the-irish-who-j
oined-british-army/.

Find & Connect Web Resource Project, The University of
Melbourne and Australian Catholic University. "Girls Reformatory,
Magill - Organisation - Find & Connect - South Australia." Document.
Accessed November 29, 2016.
https://www.findandconnect.gov.au/ref/sa/biogs/SE00066b.htm.
————. "St Joseph's Refuge - Organisation - Find & Connect -
South Australia." Document. Accessed October 17, 2016.
https://www.findandconnect.gov.au/ref/sa/biogs/SE00042b.htm.

"Full Text of 'Historical Records of Australia.'" Accessed
October 3, 2016.
https://archive.org/stream/historicalrecord00v17aust/historicalrecord
00v17aust_djvu.txt.

"Geoff Manning- Insight into South Australian History."
Accessed August 22, 2016.
http://www.geoffmanning.net.au/html/single-essays/essay11-first-fle
et.html.

Geyer, Mary Louise. "Destitute Asylum | Adelaidia." *Adelaidia*.
Accessed October 11, 2016.
http://adelaidia.sa.gov.au/places/destitute-asylum.

"HM Prison Parkhurst." *Wikipedia, the Free Encyclopedia*,
February 9, 2016.
https://en.wikipedia.org/w/index.php?title=HM_Prison_Parkhurst&o
ldid=704011531.

"Kaurna People | SA History Hub." Accessed October 4, 2015.
http://sahistoryhub.com.au/subjects/kaurna-people.

Klaassen, Nic. "Behind the Wall - The Women of the Destitute
Asylum Adelaide 1852-1918 (Book Review)." *Flinders Ranges
Research*, unknown.
http://www.southaustralianhistory.com.au/destitute.htm.

"LATEST TELEGRAMS. - Colonial and Intercolonial South
Australia. Adelaide, March 24th. - Northern Territory Times and
Gazette (Darwin, NT : 1873 - 1927) - 28 Mar 1890." *Trove*. Accessed
September 20, 2016. http://nla.gov.au/nla.news-article3316389.

"Laundry History 1800s, Washing Clothes in the 19th Century,
Victorian and Edwardian Laundering." Accessed September 15, 2016.
http://www.oldandinteresting.com/history-of-washing-clothes.aspx.

Ltd, Allied Newspapers. "The Irish and 19th-Century British
Malta: A Rethink of Perceptions." *Times of Malta*. Accessed June 16,

2016.
http://www.timesofmalta.com/articles/view/20160410/life-features/T
he-Irish-and-19th-century-British-Malta-a-rethink-of-perceptions.60
8423.

Macquarie University, Sydney, Department of Linguistics.
"History and Accent Change," February 19, 2009.
http://clas.mq.edu.au/australian-voices/history-accent-change.

"Marriage in the 19th Century." *Spartacus Educational.*
Accessed May 27, 2016.
http://spartacus-educational.com/Wmarriage.htm.

"Measuring Worth - Purchasing Power of the Pound." Accessed
October 7, 2016. https://www.measuringworth.com/ukcompare/.

Painter, Alison. "19 March 1849 Destitute Asylum." *SA 175*
(Professional Historians Association (SA). Accessed December 31,
2015.
http://www.sahistorians.org.au/175/chronology/march/19-march-184
9-destitute-asylum.shtml.

Pathé, British. "House At Colchester Damaged." Accessed
December 9, 2016.
http://www.britishpathe.com/video/house-at-colchester-damaged/que
ry/bombs.

Perkins, Roberta. "Control, Regulation and Legislation."
Monograph chapter. Accessed March 23, 2016.
http://www.aic.gov.au/publications/previous%20series/lcj/1-20/work
ing/chapter%202%20%20control%20regulation%20and%20legislati
on.html.

Read, Julian. "Colchester Memories." *Essex Life.* Accessed
December 9, 2016.
http://www.essexlifemag.co.uk/out-about/places/colchester_memorie
s_1_3588763.

"SA Memory." Accessed November 2, 2015.
http://www.samemory.sa.gov.au/site/page.cfm?c=1320&mode=singl
eImage.

"Saint Patrick's Church | SA History Hub." Accessed October 4,
2015. http://sahistoryhub.com.au/places/saint-patricks-church.

THQ, The Salvation Army Australia Eastern Territory.
"Australian Beginnings » Salvos.org.au/emerald/." Text. Accessed
December 6, 2016.
https://salvos.org.au/emerald/our-history/australian-beginnings/.

"Second Boer War." *Wikipedia*, December 4, 2016.
https://en.wikipedia.org/w/index.php?title=Second_Boer_War&oldid
=753005787.

"The Widow & the Law: A Brief History of Widows' Pensions in
Britain." *Dr Nadine Muller*, August 20, 2014.
http://www.nadinemuller.org.uk/research/the-widow-and-the-law/ .

"TIMELINE 1834-1851 - PIONEERS & SETTLERS BOUND
FOR SOUTH AUSTRALIA." Accessed August 22, 2016.
http://www.slsa.sa.gov.au/fh/passengerlists/South%20Australian%20
Timeline%201834-51.htm.

"Victorian & Edwardian Services (Houses) 1850-1914."
Accessed September 16, 2016.
http://fet.uwe.ac.uk/conweb/house_ages/services/print.htm.

"Voluntary Aid Detachment." *Wikipedia*, November 4, 2016.
https://en.wikipedia.org/w/index.php?title=Voluntary_Aid_Detachm
ent&oldid=747779044.

"Water in South Australia's Early Days." Accessed August 22,
2016. http://www.familyhistorysa.info/sahistory/water.html.

Wilson, Georgia. "The Beginnings of 'Australian English.'" Text.
ABC News, March 16, 2015.
http://www.abc.net.au/news/2015-03-16/the-story-behind-'australian
-english'/6315078.

"Women and the Victorian Regiment." *The Social Historian*.
Accessed January 18, 2016.
http://www.thesocialhistorian.com/women-and-the-victorian-regime
nt/.

Newspaper articles (used for background)

"CURRIE STREET IN THE SIXTIES. - Observer (Adelaide, SA :
1905 - 1931) - 23 Feb 1918." *Trove*. Accessed October 3, 2016.
http://nla.gov.au/nla.news-article164147864.

"CURRIE STREET IN THE SIXTIES. - The Register (Adelaide,
SA : 1901 - 1929) - 14 Feb 1918." *Trove*. Accessed June 20, 2016.
http://nla.gov.au/nla.news-article60335793.

"EMIGRANTS FROM IRELAND TO SOUTH AUSTRALIA. -
TO E. L. GRUNDY, ESQ. - South Australian (Adelaide, SA : 1844 -

1851) - 14 Nov 1850." *Trove*. Accessed June 21, 2016.
http://nla.gov.au/nla.news-article71627608.

"English Extracts. - IRISH IMMIGRATION TO SOUTH
AUSTRALIA. - The Colonist (Sydney, NSW : 1835 - 1840) - 1 Jan
1840." *Trove*. Accessed October 4, 2016.
http://nla.gov.au/nla.news-article31724317.

"FIFTY YEARS WITH ONE FIRM. - A PIONEER'S
REMINISCENCES. - Observer (Adelaide, SA : 1905 - 1931) - 30 Apr
1910." *Trove*. Accessed June 20, 2016.
http://nla.gov.au/nla.news-article164697164.

"IRELAND. - DESTRUCTIVE FIRE IN DUBLIN. - Australian
Town and Country Journal (Sydney, NSW : 1870 - 1907) - 31 Jul
1875." *Trove*. Accessed March 5, 2016.
http://nla.gov.au/nla.news-article70584224.

"WOMEN'S UNIVERSE - WOMEN PIONEERS
REMINISCENCES OF EARLY DAYS. RELATED AT GLENELG.
- The Mail (Adelaide, SA : 1912 - 1954) - 30 Dec 1922." *Trove*.
Accessed June 20, 2016. http://nla.gov.au/nla.news-article63772979.

About the author

Stella Budrikis was born in Rochdale, Lancashire, England and migrated to Perth in Western Australia with her family as a twelve year old. She has worked as a medical practitioner, a freelance writer, a pastoral care worker, and a full time mother. She and her husband live in Perth and have two adult daughters.

She began researching her family history when her parents were turning 70, thinking it would be good to give them a printed family tree as a gift. The research has continued to be her chief pastime ever since. On her blog "Clogs and Clippers" she presents her findings and discusses the ups and downs of doing family history research, often with a dash of humour.

10234332R00113

Printed in Germany
by Amazon Distribution
GmbH, Leipzig